VGM Opportunities Series

OPPORTUNITIES IN PSYCHOLOGY CAREERS

Charles M. Super, Ph.D.
Donald E. Super, Ph.D.

Revised by
Blythe Camenson

Foreword by
Joanne E. Callan, Ph.D.
Former Executive Director—Education Directorate
American Psychological Association

Preface by
Dan Matthews, Ph.D.
Director, University of New Mexico Department of Psychology Clinic

 VGM Career Books

Library of Congress Cataloging-in-Publication Data

Super, Charles M.
    Opportunities in psychology careers / Charles M. Super, Donald E. Super ; foreword by
Joanne E. Callan.—Rev. ed. / revised by Blythe Camenson.
        p. cm. — (VGM opportunities series)
    Includes bibliographical references (p.).
    ISBN 0-658-01052-2 (hardcover)
    ISBN 0-658-01053-0 (paperback)
        1. Psychology—Vocational guidance.   I. Super, Donald E. (Donald Edwin), 1910-   II.
Camenson, Blythe.   III. Title.   IV. Series.

BF76 .S86 2001
150'.23'73—dc21

00-68502

Published by VGM Career Books
A division of The McGraw-Hill Companies.
4255 West Touhy Avenue, Lincolnwood (Chicago), Illinois 60712-1975 U.S.A.
Copyright © 2001 by The McGraw-Hill Companies.
All rights reserved. No part of this book may be reproduced, stored in a retrieval system, or
transmitted in any form or by any means, electronic, mechanical, photocopying, recording, or
otherwise, without the prior written permission of the publisher.
Printed in the United States of America
International Standard Book Number: 0-658-01052-2 (hardcover)
                                                       0-658-01053-0 (paperback)

1   2   3   4   5   6   7   8   9   0   LB/LB   0   9   8   7   6   5   4   3   2   1

CONTENTS

The three psychologies. An overview of psychology specialties.
Questions in psychology. Psychology as science. Psychology as
profession. Psychology as academic pursuit and instructional field.
Psychology and the public debate. Psychology's place in society.

Experimental and physiological psychology. Engineering
psychology. Developmental psychology. Educational psychology.
The psychology of personality. Social psychology. Psychometrics
and quantitative methods. Industrial and organizational psychology.
Counseling psychology. Clinical and abnormal psychology. School
psychology. Sports psychology. Emerging specialties, related fields,
and interdisciplinary bridges.

Master's degree holders. Bachelor's degree holders. Rapid growth.
Where psychologists work. Geographic distribution. Women and
minorities in psychology.

ABOUT THE AUTHORS

Charles McAfee Super is Professor of Human Development and Family Studies at the Pennsylvania State University and an Associate in Practice at the Child, Adult, and Family Psychological Center in State College, Pennsylvania. He was previously director of a program of education and therapy for parents at the Judge Baker Children's Center in Boston, where he also held academic appointments at the Harvard Medical School and the Harvard School of Public Health. He has directed or participated in research projects on early human development and family life in the Netherlands, Kenya, Zambia, Guatemala, Colombia, Haiti, and Bangladesh, as well as the United States. A staff member of the 1970 White House Conference on Children, his writings have been published in psychological, anthropological, and medical journals such as *Developmental Psychology, Child Development, Medical Anthropology, Developmental Medicine and Child Neurology,* and *Social Science and Medicine.* Professor Super has contributed chapters to many books on child development and has served as consultant or committee member for the Social Science Research Council, the World Health Organization, and the United Nations Educational, Scientific, and Cultural Organization.

Donald Edwin Super, Professor Emeritus of Psychology and Education at Teachers College, Columbia University, was international coordinator of the Work Importance Study in the department of psychology at the University of Florida. Until his retirement, he also was actively affiliated with the University of Georgia and Armstrong State College (in Savannah) and served as consultant to various government agencies, corporations, and educational institutions. Professor Super has served as a consulting editor for several American, British, and international psychological journals and is the author or coauthor of such books as *Appraising Vocational Fitness, The Psychology of Careers, Computer-Assisted Counseling, Measuring Vocational Maturity,* and *Career Devel-*

opment in Britain. He has authored or coauthored several widely used psychological tests for vocational counseling and personnel selection. He is an honorary fellow of the National Institute for Careers Education and Counseling in Cambridge, and was its director for three years while a fellow at Wolfson College, Cambridge University. He is past president of international and American organizations in the fields of psychology and education, including the Division of Counseling Psychology of the American Psychological Association. In 1983 he received the American Psychological Association's Award for Distinguished Scientific Contributions to Applications of Psychology. He is also the recipient of a Doctor of Science degree from Oxford University.

This edition was revised by Blythe Camenson. Educated in Boston, Camenson earned her B.A. with a double major in psychology and English from the University of Massachusetts and her M.Ed. in counseling from Northeastern University. She worked in the mental health field for several years, then moved overseas and taught English as a foreign language in various universities in the Persian Gulf. Now based in Albuquerque, New Mexico, she is a full-time writer and director of Fiction Writer's Connection, a membership organization that helps new writers learn how to get published. Her website is at www.fictionwriters.com.

Blythe Camenson has more than three dozen books in print, most published by VGM Career Books. She is also the co-author of *Your Novel Proposal: From Creation to Contract* (Writer's Digest Books, 1999).

FOREWORD

Psychology appeals strongly to those who consider entering the field for several compelling reasons. One is its basic focus on human behavior—a topic relevant to each of us as individuals and in our many different relationships. At all ages, the psychological aspects of our behavior and that of others are key in how we perceive and experience our worlds.

Another of psychology's appeals has to do with its wide scope. Born out of both the experimental laboratory and philosophy, psychology is a science, yet it is also closely aligned with the social sciences and humanities. Psychologists may concentrate their professional activities in science, for example, conducting research from the full range of human and animal behavior. Or, they may focus on applied psychology, working with individuals, groups, institutions, and systems from various theoretical orientations. They might choose to teach psychology from high school through postdoctoral levels. Some psychologists combine two or all three of these activities at different times in their careers.

Psychology also is attractive because of its direct relevance to society. Many of the world's most pressing problems—such as crime and violence, disease prevention and treatment, lack of shelter, and ecological issues—can be best addressed through the application of psychological knowledge and research because they are tied so closely to human needs and behaviors.

In the near future, there will be increasing demand for well-educated and trained psychologists. With advancing technology and concomitant shrinking of our increasingly complex world, psychology will be called upon more and more to address individual and societal needs. In responding, it will rely on bright people with integrity and ethical sensitivity.

Joanne E. Callan, Ph.D.
Former Executive Director-Education Directorate
American Psychological Association

PREFACE

I suppose I have no greater interest in and curiosity about people than average. That's only because the average is so high. We are intensely social creatures and our desire and need to observe, know, wonder, predict, and attempt to influence or control each other is almost as strong as our hungers for food and water. We are all (with the possible exception of a couple of rare forms of psychopathology) driven to spend much of our time trying to figure each other out. So, even though I am a psychologist, I may not be more interested in people than you are. However, I have the great fortune to be able to spend my time and make my living engrossed in this basic human preoccupation.

Not surprisingly, I love what I do. My passion for learning about and interacting with others is carried out in the training clinic at a state university, the place where doctoral students in psychology learn to be therapists and to do psychological assessment. Since psychology is both the science of behavior (I was trained as a researcher) and one of the healing arts (I was trained also to listen, understand, and use my empathy) I have to (and get to) keep up as well as I can in two separate but related areas. To teach I have constantly to learn. I learn from reading, observing, and living. Plus, I say without apology, that I learn as much from my students as from any other source. And they learn from me that it's okay and good to be anxious about the work of dealing with fragile and precious people and that they can learn to use themselves and their knowledge to help others.

These days, the most exciting thing I'm learning from and with my students is neuropsychology—the study of the brain and how it works. Psychologists have long been the leaders among human scientists and mental health professionals in the development and use of psychological testing to measure mental abilities and emotional characteristics. For the past couple of decades, we've also been able to see, through brain scans or neuroimages, what the brain of a living person looks like and what it's doing when engaged in various tasks. We can't see thoughts, of course, but we can see what parts of the brain "light up" when a person's doing a particular type of thinking. And, we can look at people with different diagnoses or normal individuals with different results on our psychological tests and see how their brains function in different ways. Psychologists are working in teams with physicians (neurologists), radiologists, chemists, physicists, computer experts, and others to unravel mysteries about the brain, body, and behavior. The results are complex while enlightening—I once read that if the brain were simple to understand, it would be too simple to do the understanding. But it's extraordinary what we're learning.

So far, I can't say that the advances in neuropsychology and neuroimaging have changed how I do and teach psychotherapy and psychological assessment. I do understand my clients differently and often am better able to help them see how they developed some of their patterns of perceiving and living. I also have learned that the cognitive therapy that I do results in changes in brain images (brain chemistry) that are similar to what happens when the person takes some of the valuable new medications for depression.

But for now, I can enjoy the pure science of it all, because whatever I learn about people and how they think and how they deal with their emotions and relate to other people is part of what I'm supposed to do in my job. That's one of the loveliest parts of what I do—anything I read, see, experience, hear, talk about with others, feel, or find inside myself can become part of my work, if I spend the time to reflect on it and develop my understanding. Even my own weaknesses provide valuable information (and no, I haven't gotten rid of all my own weaknesses and flaws).

Psychology at its best is both the collecting of information and the application of careful methodology and reason to understand what that information means. I often describe psychology as the most skeptical of all the mental health disciplines, and I like that about it. The bookshelves are filled with self-help guides, and claims about improving the human condition are spread throughout the sections of bookstores. Psychologists (and others with a scientific approach to human problems and behavior) have helped us and will continue to help us sort through these claims and refine our thinking about how to be human and how to improve the human condition.

So, one of the promises that psychology holds for you if you study it and work with it is a different understanding of yourself, the people you meet, and human nature. I could have said "a better understanding," and that would probably be true, but I think the more honest claim is that you will come to understand people differently—more richly and complexly and deeply. But you're likely also to become more aware of what you don't know and to doubt the ways you've typically come to categorize and predict and influence others. (To be honest, there are dogmatic and arrogant psychologists who think they know it all. I, myself, find the whole endeavor profoundly humbling, while enlightening). If your teachers are successful, you'll grow in both knowledge and doubt. And in acceptance of yourself and others. That doesn't mean you'll lose your ability to believe and judge and be moral, but your morality is likely to become richer and more complex, too. I know I'm different as a person because I chose this field. (Or did it choose me?)

All this adds up to a mixed bag of values that comes out of studying psychology and doing psychology. Whether you simply take psychology courses, major in it, or do advanced work toward a master's degree or a doctorate, you will increase your knowledge, change your way of looking at and thinking about yourself and others, and simultaneously develop more questions, more doubts, and a healthy skepticism. If you're okay with ambiguity and willing to put at risk any feeling you might have in the security of your judgments, go for it. You'll never be bored.

Dan Matthews, Ph.D.
Director, University of New Mexico Department of Psychology Clinic
Albuquerque, New Mexico

ACKNOWLEDGMENTS

I would like to thank Dr. Jessica Kohout, director of the American Psychological Association's research office, for her help in providing the latest figures for this update. Her patience and cooperation should not go unnoticed.

Blythe Camenson

CHAPTER 1

PSYCHOLOGY TODAY

Most people think they have an accurate idea of what a doctor or a lawyer does, and they are probably right. Most people will admit, however, that they have no idea what a mycologist is, although the field of mycology is easily described as the study of fungi. People's ideas about psychology are different. Many people think they know what a psychologist is and have some idea of what a psychologist does, but many others have only a fuzzy or incorrect view about the field of psychology and the many varieties of psychological work.

For people who have been to college, psychology may be remembered as an introductory course, maybe in an area they never pursued further. Perhaps they could not see the value of studying how rats learn to run mazes, how cats get out of puzzle boxes, or how the mechanism of the eye reacts to light and darkness. None of the subject matter of the course seemed to have any bearing on self-understanding, getting along with others, or helping people with problems of living. Yet psychology is supposed to be the science of human behavior!

Today increasing numbers of people have encountered psychologists in school, industry, or the armed forces. They are likely to think of psychologists as mental testers or as the genial people in the guidance or personnel office who always had time to listen to what you thought you wanted to do. Any one of these pictures of a psychologist is good as far as it goes, but it does not go very far.

THE THREE PSYCHOLOGIES

There are three different ways of looking at what psychology is. It is an *academic discipline,* a body of knowledge with themes of method and content that tie together disparate parts. The knowledge is organized and synthesized into theories and "schools of thought" for communication among members of the scientific community and for transmittal to students and other interested parties. Thus psychologists may be teachers and writers. The way psychology's knowledge is expanded, through various methods of structured inquiry, makes psychology also a *science*. The scientist fashions questions and guidelines for finding answers to those questions. Many psychologists spend their time in a laboratory as part of a research team. Finally, psychology is also a *profession,* that is, an organized way of using the academic and scientific knowledge for the betterment of individuals and groups of individuals. Professional psychologists, in this sense, practice psychotherapy and advise business managers, plan mental health services, find effective ways to display computerized information, and diagnose children's problems in school.

No one psychologist, of course, carries out all the activities of each aspect of psychology, and the variety of combinations that people choose for their careers is part of what makes understanding the nature of psychology seem complicated at first. It is also true that some aspects of psychology are much more familiar to nonpsychologists than are others, and some of the familiar roles appear similar to other occupations.

There is, for example, a common confusion between psychologists and psychiatrists. Psychologists differ from psychiatrists partly in the content of their training and partly in the work they generally do. The differences in their training are best summed up by the different academic degrees that they are awarded upon completion of their university education. The psychiatrist earns the degree of Doctor of Medicine (M.D.) and, as a physician, has studied the biological sciences that are basic to the profession of medicine and the techniques of medical practice. More knowledge of psychiatry is acquired later in practical training and related study.

The fully trained psychologist, on the other hand, earns the degree of Doctor of Philosophy (Ph.D.), Psychology (Psy.D.), or Education (Ed.D.). (The Ph.D. is still the most common higher degree.) The psychologist has studied the biological and social sciences related to psychology and has specialized in the science of psychology as a graduate student. Preparation for an applied field may have included the study of relevant professional problems and methods. There may have been further practical training after the doctorate. This means that, like the physician who later specializes in psychiatry, the psychologist has been trained in the principles and techniques of a special field of knowledge and its supporting fields. It also means that, unlike the psychiatrist, the psychologist has been trained primarily in the behavioral sciences. Psychologists also are trained in research methods that enable them to add to their store of knowledge.

Psychology is both a science and a profession. As a science, psychology is the study of how people perceive, think, feel, and act; as a profession, it is concerned with predicting how people will act, helping people to modify their behavior and helping organizations and even communities and societies to change. This means that a psychologist may spend time in research, which adds to our knowledge of behavior and develops new ways of understanding behavior, or helps people and institutions change their behavior, structure, or functions. Or the psychologist may spend more time working with people, studying them by examining records of what they have done or by talking with them in order to help them modify their behavior, change the methods of their organizations, or put their resources to better use.

Many psychologists work with people and do research. The psychologist who works with people can see firsthand the important problems to be studied and often gets better ideas of how to study them. There is a better chance that what is found out in research will be used if the researcher also works with people. For these very reasons, university programs for the professional preparation of psychologists who will work with people include a good deal of emphasis on research.

Many psychologists become scientists rather than practitioners. In this respect they are like physiologists, bacteriologists, and other natural scientists whose research results are used by physicians in the treatment of illness, or like sociologists, economists, and other social scientists, whose research knowledge is used in government, industry, and education. But many other psychologists become practitioners; that is, they put into practice the knowledge that they and their pure-scientist colleagues accumulate.

 ## AN OVERVIEW OF PSYCHOLOGY SPECIALTIES

Among specialists, there are clinical psychologists, who, in some respects, resemble psychiatrists, because they apply their knowledge of psychological principles and methods to the diagnosis and treatment of mental disorders; there are personnel psychologists, who apply their knowledge of psychological principles and methods to the study and improvement of personnel practices in industry and government; and there are school psychologists, who use their knowledge of psychological principles and techniques to help teachers understand and work more effectively with the children in their classes. They also work directly with children and their parents to help them make better adjustments to school and life in general.

In all three specialties—clinical, personnel, and school—the psychologist works in a field that is more social than biological, for the problems of personal adjustment are primarily problems of interpersonal or human relations. The clinical psychologist and the psychiatrist do have common ground in the problems of mental health, along with the psychiatric social worker and the psychiatric nurse. However, the psychiatrist has a distinctive medical contribution to make to study and treatment, and often there is a focus on illness and healing. The psychologist has a distinctive sociopsychological contribution to make, with an emphasis on changing behavior.

But clinical, personnel, and school psychologists are not the only practitioners. Today behavioral scientists—specialists in developmental psychology, personality theory, social psychology, educational psychology, and experimental psychology—find that their understanding of human behavior (and the methods they bring to bear upon its study) causes them to become increasingly involved in practice.

Most often, these behavior scientists apply their knowledge to the behavior of normal people functioning in everyday circumstances, rather than people with serious problems. Experimental psychologists find themselves involved in engineering problems in industry or in medical problems in space exploration. Educational and developmental psychologists are drawn into designing and evaluating new methods of teaching the handicapped, the normal, and the gifted. Social psychologists help plan and evaluate the outcome of government policies or political campaigns. Personality theorists may participate in any of these projects. A more in-depth look at the various specializations is provided in Chapter 2.

QUESTIONS IN PSYCHOLOGY

To round out our picture of the nature of psychology, let us consider some of the kinds of problems on which psychologists work. A discussion of some of the scientific questions studied by psychologists follows, after which some of the more practical problems on which psychologists work are reviewed. The distinction between the *scientific* and the *practical,* while convenient, is actually difficult to make and to justify. For example, the problem of the localization of brain functions is of interest not only for an understanding of human intellectual functioning, but also because it has practical importance in the rehabilitation of brain-injured people. Similarly, the practical use of tests for predicting educational or vocational success throws theoretical light on the structure of mental abilities by showing how differential aptitudes are related to significant social behavior.

PSYCHOLOGY AS SCIENCE

About one-fifth of America's psychologists are employed primarily in research. Whether their work is better called basic or applied is often difficult to decide, as the examples given here will make clear. Many psychologists employed primarily in teaching or in practice spend some time in the study of psychological problems or issues, although the questions asked, the methods used, and the types of data collected and analyzed vary widely.

The Psychology of Memory

The psychology of memory, especially for highly emotional and painful events, has long held a special interest for psychologists. A primary focus of Freud's early work, for example, was to recover adult patients' repressed memories of traumatic experiences, on the theory that these experiences held the key to patients' current suffering. He later concluded that many of the "memories" were actually fantasies—unfulfilled wishes related to "infantile sexuality" that were not permitted into the stream of normal consciousness; this was one origin of his theory of neurotic disorders. Modern findings about the frequency of child sexual abuse has raised the question now for many psychologists of whether Freud may have been too quick to hear these stories as fantasies— perhaps they were painful memories struggling to be recalled. Some therapists have thus been careful to consider all such memories by patients as potentially true unless there is strong reason to think they were fabricated or imagined.

The question of accuracy in memory is of great importance when there are allegations of sexual abuse of children. More than twenty thousand children testify each year in abuse trials, and their testimony is usually considered to be truthful and accurate unless proven otherwise. But research by Maggie Bruck at McGill University and Stephen Ceci at Cornell University have called into question even this assumption about memory. They found that persistent, repeated questioning on a particular topic over a period of several weeks can lead young children (under six years old) to "remember" events that never took place. Often child victims of suspected abuse are repeatedly asked about alleged events by a parent, the police, and case workers. But a child in the study by Ceci and his colleagues, for example, who had never been to the hospital, recounted a detailed, if somewhat disjointed, story about his visit to the hospital after being questioned about it once a week for eleven consecutive weeks. It seems that children normally construct their memories in part from what they hear from adults about their own past experiences. This new information about the way memory works in children makes interesting science, but it also makes much more difficult the job of psychologists and others who have the responsibility of investigating questions of abuse and protecting the children involved, as well as respecting the rights of the accused. Ceci and Bruck, among others, have made suggestions about improving the methods used in such investigations in order to minimize the possibility of error.

The Psychology of Learning

The physiology of learning has long been a major topic of scientific research in psychology. It was this interest that prompted much of the well-known research on rats in mazes, and some of this research tried to find out about how memories were formed in the neurons and chemicals of the brain. Another line of investigation has advanced to the point that a new technique is possible for promoting certain kinds of learning. This technique is *biofeedback,* and the learning involves deliberate control over bodily functions that were earlier thought to be uncontrollable. The principle is a simple one: The behavior to be influenced—for example, the heart rate—is monitored by an electronic device. A second piece of apparatus signals by a light or a sound when the heart is going faster or slower than some predetermined rate. The subject or patient can then learn to exercise some control over the heart rate in response to the signal. With such techniques people have been able to influence their own heart rate, blood pressure, and even the brain waves associated with different states of consciousness. Recent discoveries concerning behavioral aspects of heart disease raise new questions about the biosocial origins of such disorders and suggest new avenues of research.

Research on biofeedback illustrates both the coherence of psychology across specialties and the interplay between *pure* and *applied* science in psychology. The techniques of biofeedback were developed by psychologists with backgrounds in both physiological and experimental psychology and were quickly recognized by personality and clinical psychologists, physicians, and others as potentially useful in the treatment of some kinds of psychosomatic problems and psychological anxieties. Recently there have been promising attempts at using biofeedback as therapy for more traditional medical problems involving irregularities of the heartbeat, gastric ulcers, asthma, and epilepsy. At the same time, the results of this work are posing major new questions to other psychologists about theories of learning, psychophysiology, and personality and mental functioning.

The Structure of Mental Ability

Another question faced by psychologists has been that of the structure of mental ability. Is there such a thing as general intelligence, or is intelligence actually made up of a number of special abilities? Theory first described a number of distinct mental faculties, but intelligence tests became possible only when a French psychologist, Dr. Alfred Binet, abandoned the idea of separate faculties of mind and devised a general intelligence test. Then other psychologists, in particular the late Dr. L. L. Thurston of the University of Chicago, used improved tests, experimental designs, and statistical methods to break general intelligence into a number of primary mental abilities, the number of which continues to increase with improved methods.

The nature and nurture of intelligence continues to attract psychological researchers. Howard Gardner of Harvard University has organized evidence that there are seven "intelligences," not only the logical and linguistic skills of traditional tests, but also musical intelligence, spatial intelligence, bodily-kinesthetic intelligence, the capacity to know oneself, and the ability to understand others. In presenting his theory of multiple intelligences, Gardner draws on research from neuropsychology, developmental psychology, and metric psychology, as well as related fields in cognitive science and anthropology.

It has often been assumed that tested intelligence of a high level is genius. But research by Drs. J. P. Guilford of the University of Southern California, Paul Torrance of the University of Georgia, and Jacob W. Getzels and Philip W. Jackson of the University of Chicago have made it clear that genius consists of more than a higher level of intelligence as measured by standard tests. Real genius also requires abilities and traits that enable the individual to see the possibility of combining ideas or things in new ways and thus come up with novel solutions to problems or new uses for old materials.

Old ideas of group or racial superiority involve assumptions about the abilities of people. A number of psychologists have therefore used their knowledge and methods to study such claims. They are often joined in this work by anthropologists and sociologists. Dr. Otto Kleinberg, a psychologist who has pursued a distinguished career both at Columbia University and at the Sorbonne in Paris, compared the tested intelligence of African-Americans who remained in the South with that of African-Americans who migrated to the North. He collected substantial evidence to show that differences in environment, rather than in heredity, are the important factors underlying the differences between the intelligence test scores of African-Americans and Caucasians. Dr. Arthur Jensen has questioned some aspects of this work and urges that possible racial differences in mental functioning (which may, in fact, sometimes favor Caucasians and sometimes African-Americans) should be given intensive study. Most psychologists do not agree with his interpretations, and controversy continues unabated over the cultural, social, nutritional, and medical influences on intellectual development and performance, often fed by people who generate more heat than light.

The debate does not take place only in the ivory tower, however. Because of the controversy over the appropriate use of intelligence tests with persons from minority backgrounds, a legal suit was brought in California to prevent I.Q. tests from being used in the school placement of African-American children. Psychologists were involved in both sides of the legal argument, which eventually resulted in a court injunction against using I.Q. data to place minority children in special education classes.

The Development of Morality

Some people develop a strong sense of conscience while others are not so sensitive to right and wrong. Some people are more helpful than others. Why? These questions have interested psychologists for a long time, just as they have challenged philosophers, sociologists, and many others. In order to answer such questions, personality psychologists have studied how different types of families teach morality and social values; developmental psychologists have investigated how children of different ages think about moral questions and how they respond to the needs of others; and social psychologists have collected and analyzed data on how group pressures and situational factors affect moral behavior. Everyday life makes it obvious that no one has yet learned how to make everyone perfect, but useful ideas have been developed about how to encourage the learning of constructive, helpful behavior. This continues to be a lively field of research, especially as psychologists, like many other citizens, respond to what they see as ethical problems related to war, violent crime, deceitful behavior in business and politics, and other ills that are as numerous today as they were in ancient society. Some of the most recent applications of these related bodies of work are taking place in preventive programs for school-age children. One program in New Haven, Connecticut, combines principles developed in cognitive psychology, child development, and "person-centered" therapy to promote social competence through a school-based program. Educational and community psychologists in a number of cities are working on similar programs to help children acquire the social and behavioral skills that may help them avoid the dangers of drug abuse, teenage pregnancy, and AIDS, as well as encourage constructive activity for the benefit of themselves and their communities.

PSYCHOLOGY AS PROFESSION

Half of America's psychologists are employed primarily in professional activities, putting psychological knowledge to work in everyday life. Psychologists often are thought of as test specialists, and many of them are. One of the largest testing organizations is the Educational Testing Service, headquartered in Princeton, New Jersey. Its staff members develop tests that aid in the selection and guidance of students in college and various professional schools. They also conduct research in the development of new types of tests for educational selection and evaluation. The armed forces, the United States Civil Service Commission, and many business and industrial organizations have similar staffs of psychologists working on problems of testing and related procedures for personnel selection and classification. Increasing awareness of the inappropriateness of some tests for minority group members, specifically tests that are based on the common experiences of majority group members, has made such applications both more difficult and more important.

Assessment and Counseling

Assessment and counseling are other common functions of psychologists, in which the psychologist works with students or adult clients to help them achieve better self-understanding, to make wise plans, and to take steps toward self-fulfillment in college, at work, in the home, and in the use of leisure time.

The diagnosis and modification of behavior, as well as emotional and intellectual disorders, also are functions performed by psychologists. Psychologists working in schools, psychological clinics, mental hygiene clinics, and hospitals study children and adults by means of tests, play techniques, and interviews to better understand their behavior. They also help these people to modify their behavior by using various techniques of play, discussion, and work.

Most often this work is carried out with careful planning in appropriately designed institutions, but sometimes psychologists are called to help in unusual crises. In 1987, for example, there was a major airplane crash in Detroit that killed 153 people. A vice-president of the airline, which had a twenty-five-year record of safety until then, asked James Butcher at the University of Minnesota to organize immediate mental health counseling for employees and victims' families. In the next ten days approximately twelve hundred people in six cities around the country were helped with the problems of depression, traumatic loss, guilt, and anger. Individually and in groups, in offices, airport crew lounges, and over the telephone, psychologists began a course of work that dealt with the tragedy in an immediate and effective way in an unusual collaboration of corporation and university.

Training and Group Processes

Psychologists help people not only through counseling and clinical work, but also through the analysis and improvement of group procedures, interpersonal relations, and organizational functioning. For example, Dr. Alfred Marrow, textile corporation president and industrial psychologist, became interested in what effects would be achieved if workers discussed plans for new company policies before they are made, as contrasted with setting policies and then telling workers about them. He asked psychologists of the Research Center for Group Dynamics, located at the University of Michigan, to conduct an experiment in one of his plants in order to test these two methods of decision making. The experiment showed more complete acceptance of policy changes and more wholehearted cooperation when decision making was preceded by worker discussion of facts and issues. Many consulting and some staff psychologists now help industry use these methods.

The improvement of training or educational methods is an important area of applied psychology. Many city school systems and universities have bureaus of educational research, which employ educational psychologists. These people work on problems of instructional methods, the organization of subject matter, and the evaluation of instruction.

When training problems arise, whether in schools, colleges, business, industry, government, or the armed forces, they may be solved by non-psychologist practitioners, such as teachers, personnel people, and others on the basis of general psychological knowledge or experience. On the other hand, they may be solved with the assistance of psychologists who are more expert in the psychology of learning and more experienced in designing methods of ascertaining how well methods actually work.

Not only do psychologists study, devise, and improve methods of training, they also work on methods of doing the work itself. Engineering psychologists, like industrial engineers, work on such problems as the flow of work and arrangement of the work area, the sequence of movements and processes, and the design of the machine in relation to the person who must operate it. Because of their knowledge of human abilities and behavior, combined with training in experimental methods, psychologists are in a position to make a special contribution to the adaptation of the machine to the worker, as well as to the selection of the person for the machine.

How individuals learn to work in groups has long been a topic of applied psychological research. As with many other topics in psychology, this one was given a strong start by the needs of the military during World War II. The effective team functioning of bomber crews under combat conditions was often critical to their success and survival. In order to know better how to train crews—indeed, what to train them for—their interactions during training and combat were studied. This was done to ascertain the characteristics of effective and ineffective groups, the characteristics and behavior of the members of each of these types of groups, and the factors that make for the emergence and exercise of successful leadership. The eventual success of this work significantly facilitated the training of air crews and saved many lives. This kind of work continues. Several incidents during the Persian Gulf War, for example, prompted a new task force for studying decision making under conditions of extreme stress. Work at the Human Factors Division of the Naval Training Systems Center in Orlando, Florida, has focused attention on the "mental models" used by team members and how the coordination of their understanding of each other's jobs can minimize costly or fatal errors in communication at critical moments.

Survey Techniques

The techniques of market research and public opinion polling are further examples of the application of psychological techniques. Many psychologists are employed in consulting organizations, advertising agencies, and survey centers, conducting studies of what the consumer wants and of what the public thinks about various issues. Designing questions that will get meaningful answers, conducting surveys in ways that will get cooperation and a true sample of the public, and interpreting findings are activities that call for psychological training and skill. It has been shown, for example, that opinion pollsters who use interview methods are more likely to get frank responses if they are on the same social level and of the same race as the person they are interviewing.

PSYCHOLOGY AS ACADEMIC PURSUIT AND INSTRUCTIONAL FIELD

Many psychologists—about one-fifth of them—are primarily teachers. A generation ago, more than half of America's psychologists were primarily teachers, but research organizations and practice have absorbed the increasing numbers of young people who are entering the profession. Although psychology is being introduced as a subject of study in increasing numbers at high schools, the great majority of teaching psychologists are employed in colleges and universities.

In high schools, community colleges, and liberal arts colleges, the psychology instructor is concerned largely with the general educational value of psychology for all students, in the belief that a better understanding of human behavior will be beneficial to everyone. In professional schools, psychology professors are concerned with helping future and actual physicians, social workers, engineers, librarians, teachers, businesspeople, and others understand and master appropriate psychological principles and techniques. In graduate schools, psychology professors are concerned with the training of other psychologists for teaching, research, and professional applications or practice. Emphasis varies from one graduate school to another and even from one program to another in the same psychology department, such as from a physiological program to an organizational program.

PSYCHOLOGY AND THE PUBLIC DEBATE

The results of psychological research are increasingly being applied to public debates and the policy making in legislatures, executive offices, courtrooms, school boards, and other arenas where competing ideas about social reality and what to do about it come together. Nowhere is this more evident than in discussions concerning new federal policies for children and families. For example, Donna E. Shalala, Secretary of the Department of Health and Human Services, has written and lectured extensively on the future of America's children. In the quarterly newsletter of the Child, Youth, and Family Services Division of the American Psychological Association (Summer, 1993), Dr. Shalala discussed several areas of government action: family leave (to provide job security to parents who must take time off from work for the birth of a child, for example); child maltreatment; welfare reform; the Head Start program; and health care. On each of these topics there is psychological and behavioral research documenting the scope of the problems and the effectiveness (or lack thereof) of various interventions. The Head Start program, for example, was cited as "an American success story" for its "proven record of giving children the foundation they need for long-term success." The program was initiated in part because of the concerns of psychologists and educators in the 1960s; it was modeled on experimental programs designed by them. The first director of the Office for Children, which started the program, was Professor Edward Zigler, a psychologist on leave from Yale University, and the "proven record" Dr. Shalala cites consists largely of tests and observations compiled by psychological and behavioral researchers. This work has demonstrated so effectively the educational, social, health, and economic benefits of such programs—when they are carried out—that Head Start now enjoys the strong support of legislators and citizens from all political parties and across nearly all philosophies of government.

Sometimes in the process of policy formation psychologists are asked to provide expert testimony to lawmakers or other officials. Dr. Ellen Greenberger of the University of California at Irvine had one such experience. The Subcommittee on Labor Standards of the House of Representatives was considering a proposal by President Reagan's administration to expand the number of hours that school-age children could be legally employed. The proposal was part of Reagan's larger program to minimize federal regulations in the national economy. It was opposed by labor organizations, partly for job-security reasons, and by many who were concerned that the temptation of even minimum-wage jobs would interfere with some children's attention to properly completing their education. Dr. Greenberger had recently completed a large study of high school students and was able to present to the subcommittee factual data relevant to their debate. In her work she found that fourteen and fifteen-year-olds who worked long hours at outside jobs (fifteen hours a week or more), spent less time on homework, received lower grades, enjoyed school less, were less likely to eat dinner with their families, felt less close to their families, and used more of such substances as tobacco, alcohol, and marijuana. As she presented these results to lawmakers, Dr. Greenberger was careful to point out that the associations she found did not necessarily prove causation, but she was able to bring into her testimony other research findings and considerations that, together, were effective in helping the committee members come to their own conclusions regarding the advisability of the new proposal, which, in the end, was defeated.

The topics of public debate addressed by psychological and behavioral research are innumerable. They include issues such as recycling used materials; discrimination in the workplace; promoting healthy behaviors, especially for those at high risk; the proper role of eyewitness testimony; the alleged preventive effects of capital punishment; as well as the more traditional topics of mental health and educational reform. The recent growth of applying research results to policy matters reflects several trends. One is simply the accumulation of a much larger body of knowledge than was available in previous decades. This in turn is partly the result of the growing number of psychologists and other behavioral scientists who have been trained in research. In addition, a number of people and organizations (such as the American Psychological Association) have made extensive efforts to bring this knowledge to the attention of relevant groups of decision makers. Finally, the trend probably also reflects the increasing sophistication of the American public and their representatives with regard to the possibility of understanding human behavior through scientific research.

PSYCHOLOGY'S PLACE IN SOCIETY

By now, it should be clear that psychology has an important place, or perhaps many important places, in society. Psychology's place is wherever there are people, for wherever there are people there are problems of organization, performance, and adjustment. Wherever there are people there are problems of how to live and work together, how to learn or how to function, and how to live with oneself.

Increased awareness of these problems generally means increased willingness to provide funds for understanding and treating them. To solve all of these problems, psychologists can contribute relevant principles for the guidance of policy or for decision making, techniques of investigation to get a better understanding of the problem or for the evaluation of methods and results, and assistance in devising and trying out solutions.

CHAPTER 2

SPECIALIZATIONS IN PSYCHOLOGY

As was pointed out earlier, psychology is somewhat unusual in that it is both a science and a profession. Some psychologists are primarily scientists, engaged in research work and perhaps in related administrative and teaching activities. Others are primarily practitioners, engaged in the application of psychology to practical problems of education, business, industry, health, welfare, and everyday living. Although many of the scientists also apply their knowledge of principles and methods, and many practitioners carry on research, psychologists generally can be characterized according to one of these functions.

Moreover, there is further specialization within the field of psychology just as there is within the fields of physics and medicine. Just as the science of physics can be divided into specialties, such as astrophysics and nuclear physics, so the science of psychology can be divided into specialties, such as *experimental psychology, physiological psychology, developmental psychology, personality, social psychology, abnormal psychology,* and *psychometrics* or *measurement.* Just as the profession of medicine is divided into specialties, such as pediatrics and internal medicine, so the profession of psychology is divided into specialties, such as *clinical, counseling, school, engineering, personnel,* and *applied social psychology* (market research, propaganda, advertising, public opinion, morale, group dynamics).

The American Psychological Association (APA) currently lists fifty-two different divisions that represent the various specialized areas in the field of psychology.*

1. Society for General Psychology
2. Society for the Teaching of Psychology
3. Experimental Psychology

---

*Reprinted with permission of the American Psychological Association.

4. There is no Division 4
5. Evaluation, Measurement, and Statistics
- 6. Behavioral Neuroscience and Comparative Psychology
- 7. Developmental Psychology
8. Society for Personality and Social Psychology
9. Society for the Psychological Study of Social Issues—SPSSI
- 10. Psychology and the Arts
11. There is no Division 11
12. Society of Clinical Psychology
13. Consulting Psychology
14. Society for Industrial and Organizational Psychology
15. Educational Psychology
16. School Psychology
17. Counseling Psychology
18. Psychologists in Public Service
19. Military Psychology
- 20. Adult Development and Aging
21. Applied Experimental and Engineering Psychology
- 22. Rehabilitation Psychology
23. Society for Consumer Psychology
- 24. Theoretical and Philosophical Psychology
- 25. Experimental Analysis of Behavior
26. History of Psychology
- 27. Society for Community Research and Action: Division of Community Psychology
28. Psychopharmacology and Substance Abuse
29. Psychotherapy
- 30. Psychological Hypnosis
31. State Psychological Association Affairs
32. Humanistic Psychology
33. Mental Retardation and Developmental Disabilities
- 34. Population and Environmental Psychology
35. Society for the Psychology of Women
36. Psychology of Religion
37. Child, Youth, and Family Services
- 38. Health Psychology
39. Psychoanalysis
- 40. Clinical Neuropsychology

41. American Psychology-Law Society
42. Psychologists in Independent Practice
43. Family Psychology
44. Society for the Psychological Study of Lesbian, Gay, and Bisexual Issues
45. Society for the Psychological Study of Ethnic Minority Issues
46. Media Psychology
47. Exercise and Sport Psychology
48. Society for the Study of Peace, Conflict, and Violence: Peace Psychology Division
49. Group Psychology and Group Psychotherapy
50. Addictions
51. Society for the Psychological Study of Men and Masculinity
52. International Psychology
53. Clinical Child Psychology
54. Society of Pediatric Psychology

In this chapter we discuss more than a dozen of these fields in detail to give you an idea of the duties, qualifications, places of employment, and prospects of both doctorate and master's level psychologists in each of these specialties. It is well worth a visit, though, to the APA website to see their complete specialization information, as well as career information for psychology students (www.apa.org).

The focus of this chapter on specialties within psychology might leave the impression that psychology is a field of specialties differing from each other and lacking common ground. This impression is incorrect. The American Psychological Association's Education and Training Board, other such committees, and most departments of psychology have emphasized the importance of a firm grounding in the field of general psychology. The object here is to underline the *unity* of psychology while pointing out its special fields.

It also should be noted that the particular divisions of psychology used as subfields are to some extent arbitrary and are the outcome of historical—rather than purely logical—factors. In fact, the subfields, like psychology as a whole, are constantly growing and changing, sometimes redefining themselves or combining so closely with other trends as to become something new. The specialties listed here, however, are commonly recognized ones at present, and serve as a good orientation to the larger profession.

EXPERIMENTAL AND PHYSIOLOGICAL PSYCHOLOGY

The fields of experimental and physiological psychology were once the dominant areas of specialization in many psychology departments. However, with the growth of health service provider specialties and other fields, such as social and developmental, their role has changed in several ways. The experimental method remains an important tool in all areas of psychological science, but experimental psychology as a subfield—with its focus on sensation, perception, and learning—has not grown in recent decades with the vigor of some other fields. This is partly because some of the newer areas also depend on other approaches to the collection and analysis of data (for example, one cannot easily conduct experiments on long-term questions about personality development in children). On the other hand, physiological psychology—often now called psychobiology or neuropsychology—has prospered dramatically as it draws on and contributes to new techniques and discoveries in biology, neurology, and endocrinology. The experimental method remains at the core of this field, and the two areas—experimental and physiological—are now often considered to be one.

Experimental Psychology

The field of experimental psychology is concerned with the processes of sensation, perception, learning, and motivation. It studies problems of seeing, hearing, feeling, perceiving, learning, and wanting. These can best be studied in a laboratory situation and are basic to an understanding of the processes of knowing, thinking, judging, and problem solving. Experiments in the field of perception and cognition have made important contributions to both theory and practice in psychology.

The work of experimental psychologists may involve studying how people attend to and use different kinds of visual and auditory information as well as how this processing of information is affected by what they are looking or listening for. They also may study the differences in thinking between novices and masters in chess; the ways that rats learn to depend on their own efforts or on the efforts of others in getting food from a vending machine; the effect of the judgments of others on an individual's own judgment of the size of an object; or the effects of two different arrangements of aircraft controls on pilot performance.

The training of experimental psychologists emphasizes undergraduate preparation in mathematics and the natural sciences, including physics, chemistry, and physiology. In graduate school, the stress is on experimental methods, sense organ functions, analysis of the learning process, and on the theories related to these. Much time is spent in designing and conducting experiments as well as in constructing or becoming familiar with the laboratory apparatus that is to be used. Some preparation in developmental, educational, abnormal, cognitive, or personnel psychology or in personality theory usually is included. This is done to increase the range of problem areas in which the experimental psychologist may conduct research as well as to prepare the psychologist to teach the variety of courses usually required of instructors in small colleges and universities. Preparation below the doctorate generally is considered inadequate for experimental psychology except in some lower level positions, and these usually are held by persons working toward their doctorates.

Physiological Psychology

Physiological psychology is the study of how the physiology and anatomy of the brain, its neural network, and the hormonal system it interacts with control behavior, from eating and sex to reading and solving puzzles and caring about other people. For obvious ethical reasons, most of this work is carried out on animals, usually rats, cats, and monkeys. (Thus some of this work is called "comparative psychology," where the results from different species can be compared.) Occasionally, however, an accident in which a person's nervous system is damaged in a certain way, or an unusual case requiring neurosurgery, will stimulate an important discovery in human physiological psychology.

Research on brain function has always involved psychologists with specialists in such other fields as neurology, pharmacology, endocrinology, biology, and ethology. All of these are rapidly growing fields, and physiological psychologists contribute by working on issues that tie them together. Indeed, subspecialties now can be identified in neuropsychology, psychopharmacology, and other hybrid areas. Much of the early work in physiological psychology focused on the control of eating and drinking behavior in dogs and cats and added to general knowledge of how the nervous system senses the body's needs and directs their fulfillment. Recent work has tended to be in areas more obviously psychological, such as how the nervous systems of different species of animals facilitate certain kinds of learning that are particularly relevant for their survival, or exactly what the brain does as it constructs ideas from patches of black ink on white paper. Another rapidly growing area is called psychoneuroendocrinology, where researchers study the interactions of personality, stress, bodily functions, and disease. The techniques of such research range from surgery to carefully controlled environments, from simple observation to elegantly designed experiments.

The graduate training of a physiological psychologist naturally emphasizes the study of neuroanatomy, neurochemistry, animal behavior, and laboratory techniques. Usually students work on their research with assistance from one or two professors. A fortunate undergraduate may have the opportunity to help in a professor's research, but more often his or her preparation consists of course work in biology and chemistry, preferably also physics and electronics, and supplementing courses in experimental psychology, personality theory, learning, and motivation.

The divisions of physiological, comparative, and experimental psychology are some of the fastest growing areas. A recent survey suggests that more than two-thirds of psychologists in these specializations are employed in colleges and universities, where they teach and conduct research. Some experimental and physiological psychologists work for federal, state, or foundation research projects. Applied experimental psychologists work in the field of engineering psychology in universities and consulting organizations that have military or industrial contracts or in government or industrial organizations.

ENGINEERING PSYCHOLOGY

Most engineering psychologists work in industry, generally as engineering or "human factors" psychologists, but many are employed by the government. The Navy employs them in research positions in the Office of Naval Research and in other such installations. The Air Force employs a number who work on the design of equipment appropriate to human capacities.

Business and industry as well as the military have benefited from recognition of what applied experimental psychology can contribute to the design and use of equipment through the "human factors" approach. It is not only military and spacecraft that present problems of the arrangement and illumination of instruments and control panels, but also commercial aircraft, automobiles, typewriters, and computers; all have problems of access and control. In the case of computers, for example, there are questions of brightness and contrast in the displays of monitors. What characteristics cause problems of operator fatigue, and what kind of lighting best combines visibility with restfulness? The arrangement of the different types of office machines for their most effective use in transcription, reproduction, and distribution has been another topic of applied research by human factors psychologists. They sometimes team with personnel and organizational psychologists who focus more on individuals and groups than on equipment.

There are consulting firms that specialize in contract work of this type, often coordinating with manufacturers' staff psychologists. To the surprise of some experimental psychologists, applied experimental or engineering psychology became, during the two decades following World War II, a "demand" field, but there is now no major shortage of qualified persons because of lessened demand in industry, government, and universities. Only a small percentage of psychologists identify themselves as engineering psychologists.

Engineering psychology now has emerged as a distinct field, with preparation similar to that of experimental psychology but stressing industrial and military equipment and methods—human factors applications. Training is usually for the Ph.D., with work in experimental psychology supplemented by organizational and personnel psychology.

Although not numerous, engineering and human factors psychologists have developed considerable *esprit de corps*. In some metropolitan areas, they meet regularly for the exchange of information about research problems, methods, and applications.

DEVELOPMENTAL PSYCHOLOGY

This field of psychology often is divided into the special areas of infant, child, adolescent, adult, and old-age psychology, the last-named field being known as *gerontology*. These specialties are increasingly linked together as life-span developmental psychology. The field is concerned with growth and development from the beginning of life until death; because of the importance of the formative years, it generally has concentrated on infancy, childhood, and adolescence. In recent years, however, there has been increasing interest in the physiological, psychological, and adaptive problems of maturity and old age.

Child psychologists have studied children's intellectual and emotional development, reasoning, moral concepts, the beginnings of social behavior in infancy, the development of language, the process of socialization (learning society's valued attitudes and behaviors), the origins of attitudes toward self and others, awareness of the self, the effects of day care, and many other aspects of development. Such knowledge is important because it provides an understanding of the origins of behavior and processes of growth and contributes to the planning of programs of child rearing, education, and recreation.

Students of the psychology of adolescence have been concerned with similar problems at a higher age level. Thus, at this age level they are concerned with developmental tasks of adolescence such as advancing toward intellectual maturity, developing emotional independence of the home and family, making the transition from economic dependence on the home to being a self-sustaining and responsible individual in adult society, and approaching courtship and marriage.

Developmental psychologists concerned with adulthood have studied the adjustments typical of the prime of life, including the problems that confront people whose children have grown up and left home and those of men and women who, in mid-career, find themselves questioning their roles and their goals. Psychologists interested in old age have been concerned with the aging process, the effects of aging on the self-concept, the effects of retirement, the relationship between pattern of life and work before retirement, the nature of the changes taking place in aptitudes and interests in old age, and other similar questions.

Many of the questions asked by developmental psychologists have implications for programs and policies in institutions such as hospitals and schools as well as more widely in the community. Those who are particularly interested in these issues have begun to conceptualize a new subdiscipline of "applied developmental psychology" to focus efforts toward a developmental perspective on challenges such as minimizing the distress of hospitalized children, promoting healthy parent-child relations, and preventing teenage drug abuse and violence.

The developmental psychologist may conduct research in hospital newborn nurseries, day care centers, elementary or high schools, adult education centers, and homes for the aged. Playgrounds, scout meetings, a street corner meeting place, or a sandlot baseball field may also provide the locale for research. The developmental psychologist only rarely works in industry and is more often found in the community at large or in a specially equipped university laboratory.

The training of developmental psychologists includes the usual core studies in general, and experimental and theoretical psychology. Some of these courses may be taken at the undergraduate level together with work in biology, sociology, and cultural anthropology. In addition, the developmental psychologist will take specialized courses in the psychology of childhood and adolescence and the psychological problems of adulthood and old age, supported by considerable work in personality, theoretical, educational, and social psychology. Observational methods, measurements, and fieldwork also play an important part in training. The doctorate is necessary for employment above the assistant or technician level.

Developmental psychologists are often employed in colleges and universities, particularly in departments of education and teachers' colleges. Their principal function is teaching, although they may conduct research either as part of their work or on their own. Developmental psychologists also hold research positions in institutes devoted to child welfare, old age, or educational research. These institutes frequently are attached to universities, such as the Universities of Iowa, Minnesota, Florida, and California. Developmental psychologists may work in research laboratories connected with hospitals or homes for the aged. There also have been openings in parent education work and in writing and editing.

The emphasis on understanding infant, child, and adolescent development has led to a demand for psychologists with this type of training. The study of infants at risk from particular problems has linked developmental psychology to pediatrics. Interest in the educational implications of the theories of Jean Piaget and more recent cognitive studies has made for a greater relationship between child, experimental, and educational psychology. There is renewed concern with adult development, joining not only developmental psychology with other specialties such as personality psychology and counseling, but also academic insights with business and management. And finally, a growing elderly population has promoted greater interest in their functioning and needs.

New Doctorates in Psychology by Subfield: 1997

Seventy percent of new doctorate recipients earned degrees in the health service provider subfields—clinical, counseling, school, and other practice-related subfields. Thirty percent of new doctorates were earned in a variety of research fields. The largest single proportion of new doctorates work in human service settings (hospitals and clinics, etc.) followed by higher education.

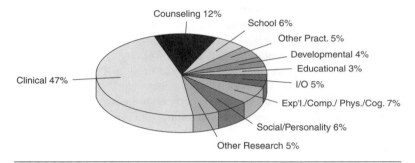

Source: Draft Preliminary Data. 1997 Doctorate Employment Survey, APA Research Office, 1999. *Note.* These data include both Ph.D.s and Psy.D.s.

EDUCATIONAL PSYCHOLOGY

The field of educational psychology is not easy to define, for while it is concerned with some problems that are most appropriately its own, it partly overlaps certain other fields. A number of specialty fields, such as measurement, counseling, and school psychology, have largely broken away from it. Remaining in it are teaching and research in the psychological problems of the educational process. Human learning is one of the primary interests of the educational psychologist as is the field of individual differences in abilities and interests. Both of these are obviously basic to education. Also basic to education is (a) developmental psychology, because education is concerned with guiding and promoting development; (b) social psychology, because children and adolescents are social creatures; and (c) the psychology of personality, because education is concerned with the development of the whole person, with adjustment as well as with the acquisition of skills.

When the educational psychologist applies his or her knowledge to individual children or adults, he or she draws on the knowledge and techniques of the school psychologist, the counseling psychologist, or the clinical psychologist. The distinguishing characteristic of the educational psychologist is a primary concern for psychological principles and techniques that have significance for educational problems. The educational psychologist is a student of educational problems, such as ability grouping and the education of the gifted, the handicapped, and the disadvantaged. A primary interest is in the implications of such problems as they relate to educational policies and processes.

It is clear that the educational psychologist must be a well-trained scientific and professional worker. Undergraduate work should be broad, stressing education and the social sciences. Good grounding in the basic fields of psychology—particularly learning theory—is essential as is advanced work in developmental psychology, social psychology, personality theory, and measurement, including courses in which these fields are drawn together and applied to education.

The educational psychologist must be familiar with the principles and techniques of counseling and guidance, have some orientation toward clinical psychology, and be very competent in evaluation and measurement. It is desirable to have acquired some competence and experience as a practitioner in one of these fields and to be familiar with a variety of educational institutions and programs.

Research training and experimental design are especially important in this field. However, of crucial importance is the ability to understand classroom problems and communicate about these with teachers and administrators. This can come only with experience gained as a classroom teacher before, during, or after advanced study. Without this understanding, the psychologist's influence probably will not be significant.

Educational psychologists usually work in colleges and universities or in city, county, state, and federal boards of education. In colleges and universities, they are engaged in teaching educational psychology, measurement, individual differences, mental health, and related courses to prospective teachers and to teachers already in service. They also frequently supervise and conduct research with graduate students or a research institute.

In school systems, educational psychologists generally are employed in research bureaus. Here they may conduct routine operations in studying the abilities and achievements of pupils or, with increasing frequency, plan and carry out—cooperatively with curriculum and instruction specialists—studies in various methods of organizing and conducting classroom work.

The growth of developmental and counseling psychology, combined with the emphasis on mental health and on clinical psychology, has left educational psychologists somewhat uncertain as to the extent of their field and the nature of their contribution. Some have stressed theory and have thus identified with developmental psychology or learning theory. Others with more applied interests have tended to become measurement specialists, mental health workers, or counseling psychologists. Still others have directed their knowledge and skills into the field of curriculum development and instruction.

There are indications that what is now—in a strict sense—the field of educational psychology may subdivide into two specialties. One specialty will be concerned with the development of learning abilities, an area that is basic to educational philosophy and methods. The other specialty will be primarily interested in new ideas and in the ways and means of getting these innovations into the mainstream of educational practice. Both instructors and research workers have been finding challenging opportunities in these areas in recent years, not only at the doctoral level, but also at the M.A. level in positions as research assistants. Recent reductions in federal funding of educational research and innovation have reduced the number of such opportunities, but have not eliminated them.

THE PSYCHOLOGY OF PERSONALITY

The field of personality, either as a research area or as a focus of attention in educational and clinical practice, remains a popular and active field of psychology today. A large number of students in graduate schools take courses and specialize in this field. In addition, many psychologists originally trained in other specialties have shifted their attention to this field and the kindred applied field of clinical psychology. With social psychology and psychometrics, the psychology of personality is the main area of scholarship and investigation basic to such service fields as clinical, counseling, and school psychology. There is much research going on in the psychology of personality, and many books are being published on this vital subject.

While psychologists historically have had some interest in the organic or physical bases of personality, their major concern in recent years has turned to its social aspects. They have studied the ways in which behavior is learned; the processes of conditioning and perception as they affect personality growth and functioning; the development of self-awareness and the enhancement and defense of the self; the influences on personality of various kinds of group memberships; the relationship between personality and culture; and the processes of personality integration and disintegration. Current projects in research and theory construction include the analysis of personality structure as a whole made up of interacting traits; the study of the need for selfhood as an integrative force in personality development; and investigation of the characteristic motives, perceptions, and actions by means of which a person interacts with others.

The work of the psychologist interested in personality may involve conducting research on certain narrowly defined problems, or it may concentrate on synthesizing the results of research in a variety of fields of psychology as they bear on theory of personality. Most theoretical treatises on the psychology of personality have been written by psychologists of the latter type or by theoretically inclined clinicians, in whose working lives research activities played a relatively small part. This separation of theory and research diminished somewhat during the years when research funds were made progressively more available to psychology as a field.

Personality theorists have studied the effects of infantile experience on the adult behavior of rats, the effects of social casework treatment on welfare families, the use of such drugs as alcohol and marijuana and the effects of these drugs on attitudes and behavior, and the development of selfhood as shown in school children's essays on what they like and dislike about themselves. One group of psychologists explored the characteristics of the authoritarian personality. Others have concentrated on the statistical analysis of personality ratings in attempts to determine the basic dimensions of personality. Others have tried to understand the limitations of a concept so broad as "personality," that is, to look for the predictable inconsistencies in behavior as well as the consistencies that reflect personality.

Psychologists specializing in the field of personality should have—in their undergraduate education—considerable work in both the biological and social sciences, particularly the latter. Mathematics through the study of calculus is important. A broad background in literature and history also helps give the perspective on people needed by a professional student of personality. Such preparation is more important than an extensive undergraduate background in psychology.

Graduate preparation should proceed to the doctorate and include the basic courses in psychology. These courses should stress personality theory and developmental, social, and abnormal psychology with considerable work in measurement and research methods. Supplementary work in cultural anthropology and sociology is essential. Some experience and skill in clinical and counseling methods generally has been considered useful in personality research. A period of time spent in full-time research after the completion of the doctorate is a highly desirable and increasingly common way of developing the research habits and insights necessary to continuing productivity in this important field.

Personality psychologists and social psychologists together constitute a small percentage of all doctoral psychologists. Few personality psychologists have only a master's degree. The jobs held by personality psychologists are largely in universities, involving both teaching and research responsibilities. There also are a number of positions at all professional levels in government service, such as the United States Public Health Service and the Office of Naval Research.

Some private social service agencies have established long-term research projects in personality and related areas. These sometimes are financed by grants from public funds as well as from foundations.

This is an important and established field in psychology, though not a large one as a specialty. There is much new interest in it, and there is a great need for really creative research workers and theorists trained at the highest levels. The prospects are that it will become more important as improved theory and techniques make new insights possible.

SOCIAL PSYCHOLOGY

Social psychology has been defined as the study of the interaction of individuals, of how individuals function in society and respond to the group. It is concerned with how they become socialized, how they utilize social patterns in the world about them, how they develop within themselves the social attitudes they find in family and neighborhood groups, how they participate in community life, and how they affect the personality patterns of those with whom they come in contact.

Social psychologists study such subjects as the social behavior of children, focusing on the development of different types of social interaction as children mature; the relationship of interpersonal relations in the home to interpersonal relations in school and club groups; personal and social factors related to the development of cooperative and competitive behavior; bargaining in conflict situations and international tensions; social attitudes such as bias, their origins, and their relationship to social behavior; voting habits and factors related to them; and the roles of individuals in groups, the personal and social situational factors related to these roles, and the effects of changing situations on roles.

Applied social psychology is concerned with the applications of the principles and techniques of the field to practical situations and problems. It embraces activities of such seemingly divergent nature as propaganda, housing, community organization, community attitudes and relations, advertising, market research, public opinion polling, morale, communication, and group dynamics. Although the applications are quite different, the principles and procedures underlying these activities actually overlap considerably. They all pertain to the study of groups and to the behavior of individuals in groups.

Applied social psychologists work on such problems as the study of national characteristics as a guide to psychological warfare and the maintenance of peace; the effectiveness of public relations and advertising; the analysis of consumer buying habits; public opinion; studying attitudes toward minority groups and the ways in which they are affected by living in segregated and nonsegregated neighborhoods; measuring changes in morale with changes in working conditions; ascertaining how a group learns to work as a team rather than as a collection of individuals; how members of a jury relate to each other as deliberations proceed; and devising and evaluating methods of leadership in group activities. The list of applications is long, varied, vital, and fascinating. This field is involved in business, industry, social agencies, schools, community situations, the armed forces, and in every kind of situation where groups of men and women are found.

The training of the social psychologist is somewhat similar to that of the personality psychologist described previously. There is less emphasis on abnormal psychology and on clinical and counseling principles and techniques. There is more emphasis on social interaction, the analysis of group behavior, social roles, perception, and communication processes. A period of postdoctoral experience as a full-time researcher, even when the ultimate objective is graduate-level teaching, is highly profitable and increasingly common. A person aiming at undergraduate teaching would find this less important but nonetheless helpful.

Positions in social psychology, like those in personality psychology, tend to be in universities, research institutes connected with universities, nonprofit organizations, government agencies such as the Department of Agriculture and the Department of Defense, and public opinion and market research consulting firms. The distinction between science and profession often breaks down here, some jobs in the area being largely scientific or theoretical in nature, some largely applied, and some a combination.

There has been rapid growth in this field of psychology ever since 1940, following less dramatic but solid growth during the 1930s. Social trends, such as public concern with issues of race and discrimination, environmentalism, war and peace, and the lag of social understanding behind such technical developments as the Internet and the use of atomic energy have accented the need for research, knowledge, and application in the social sciences. Social psychology therefore has come into its own. This trend can be expected to continue, and there will be a demand for able research workers, teachers, and consultants.

PSYCHOMETRICS AND QUANTITATIVE METHODS

The field of psychological measurement is one which, perhaps more than any other, has established psychology's place in the public's mind. The term *I.Q.* has become a household word, and the most common association with the word *psychological* would probably be the word *test.*

Psychometrics is the science of measuring human intellectual, emotional, and social characteristics and behavior, although the term sociometrics is more properly applied to measuring some aspects of social behavior.

The field is concerned with the identification of characteristics that can be measured and with the development of methods for measuring them. Its next concern is with the adaptation or development of statistical methods for the treatment of measurement data gathered, the refinement of measures, and the testing of their value as measures in relation to what they are supposed to measure.

The field overlaps with all of those that have been described so far, for its concern is the development of theories and the provision of instruments that can be used by these fields in their work. There are therefore metric psychologists who work in the fields of experimental, developmental, educational, personality and social, and abnormal psychology. The peculiar subject matter of psychometrics is measurement and statistical method, always with the objective of ultimate application to the content of some other field or fields, although at the particular moment the work is being done it may be strictly theoretical.

Some confusion may arise from the fact that the term *psychometrist* or even *psychometrician* is applied to technicians who use psychometric instruments and not to the psychologist who specializes in the science of psychometrics. The difference between the pursuit of the science and the application of the techniques is considerable.

Psychologists specializing in the science of measurement work on problems such as devising suitable tasks, questions, or other procedures for the evaluation of intellectual, personality, educational, or social characteristics; creating methods of combining these elements into scales or tests that differentiate between varying amounts of the characteristic in question; determining the consistency and independence of the measures obtained; and ascertaining their relationship to other characteristics and to subsequent behavior. Other quantitative psychologists devise and work with new methods for studying changes in psychological functioning over time and new programs for statistical analysis.

If the psychologists' work involves devising new types of procedures and instruments for the measurement of previously unidentifiable characteristics, they are engaged in the science of psychometrics. If, on the other hand, they are engaged in the construction of additional measures of characteristics already in existence, they belong more in the applied field. The two types of work are, of course, frequently combined. At the Educational Testing Service, for instance, some staff members work largely on the development of new types of measures or new ways of handling data, while others are concerned primarily with the production of new forms of existing tests.

Specialists in psychometrics, perhaps more than most other psychologists, may resemble the popular description of the Ph.D., one who "knows more and more about less and less," for their field is one of methodology rather than of content. However, as their methods are applied to a variety of substantive fields, those who work on applications find it essential to become very broad in interest and knowledge. Good undergraduate grounding in mathematics is essential—at least through calculus—supplemented by work in the physical, biological, and social sciences. At the graduate level there should be good grounding in basic psychology, supplemented by work in developmental, personality, social, and educational psychology, with intensive study of individual differences. They should also study various types of tests, measurement principles and methods, statistics, and mathematical statistics. Of course, a knowledge of computer applications is essential.

The field of measurement and evaluation is the applied branch of the more purely scientific field of psychometrics. Measurement psychologists are specialists in psychometrics who are more concerned with the application of existing techniques than with the theory of measurement or with the development of new kinds of statistical methods.

Applied measurement is concerned with selecting, constructing, and applying tests or other measures to problems such as finding out how effective a training program is; with constructing, applying, and evaluating tests and other devices, such as interview procedures, for the selection, evaluation, and upgrading of students or employees; and with developing tests for use in counseling and guidance. The work of measurement psychologists differs from that of specialists in psychometrics mainly in its emphasis on applications rather than on theory, and on the use of tests and test items rather than on statistical methods of treating test data.

Not many psychologists consider this their specialty, even when devoting themselves to it full-time, for they tend to view themselves as educational, industrial, or other substantive types of psychologists. In one survey, about 1 percent of psychologists gave this as their specialty; about half of these had a doctoral degree.

Metric psychologists are employed in a great variety of situations, wherever behavior has to be measured and measures have to be developed. They teach measurement courses and related subjects in colleges and universities and they work in educational and psychological research institutes connected with universities or schools. They are found in medical and social welfare research organizations that need assistance in developing and applying measures of the effectiveness of their work or in studying trends involving their service populations. They are employed in federal, state, and local government agencies concerned with selecting personnel, evaluating training, or studying attitudes. They work in business and industry in the study of personnel selection, employee morale and training, or in market and public opinion research. They find employment wherever other types of psychological specialists are found.

Jobs held by measurement psychologists are generally in the same settings as those of psychometricians. They include teaching related courses in colleges and universities. Test development and publishing companies, such as the Psychological Corporation and the Educational Testing Service, consulting firms, and research bureaus, such as those of large school systems and universities, often have measurement psychologists on their staffs to direct and carry out technical aspects of their work. There is no specialty certification by professional associations in this field.

Psychometricians and measurement specialists have made highly visible contributions to military functioning ever since the selective service tests used during World War II. Despite extensive cutting of federal, state, and local funds for education, and despite the tendency of business and industry to reduce its support for personnel research in times of recession, psychometrics continues to be a field in which there is some demand for specialists at all of the levels of postgraduate training.

As better methods of measuring characteristics are devised, more people want more things measured. Whereas psychometrics was confined largely to the laboratory or to the school or college a generation ago, it now has an important place in business, industry, government, the armed forces, medicine, and social welfare. The theoretical and applied often merge in this field, as in social psychology. A growing number of psychologists develop computer programs to help interpret test results.

Today, widespread concern for the appropriateness of standardized tests for members of minority and special groups, combined with questioning of the use of certain kinds of personal data for personnel selection, inhibits work on testing in some organizations and encourage innovative work in others.

In addition to the pressures resulting from an increased awareness of minorities and of related measurement problems, the so-called "truth-in-testing" movement has resulted in new work for measurement specialists. This consists to some extent of making sure that tests and test items can be justified logically and empirically to official bodies and to the inquiring public. This increases the need to demonstrate the usefulness of tests; to reconcile data collection with disclosure regulations, thus making the ability to answer correctly universal and nonpredictive; and to require more time from test experts in keeping the public properly informed.

The well-trained psychological measurement technician with an M.A. degree finds some demand for his or her services, and the well-educated, versatile, and personally effective metric psychologist with the doctorate is in demand and will continue to be.

INDUSTRIAL AND ORGANIZATIONAL PSYCHOLOGY

Industrial, organizational, and personnel psychology is the study of people at work and how they relate to work. The objective of this specialty—or constellation of specialties—is to develop and apply procedures that will result in the better utilization of personnel, the better functioning of organizations, and the maximum well-being of the worker. In this applied field, the principles and techniques of developmental, educational, personality, social, and measurement psychology are brought to bear on the problems of people in work situations. Also of concern to these psychologists is the human factor in production methods. The focus is on understanding the work situation, developing procedures, and applying principles and procedures necessary to the wise selection, effective placement, training, upgrading, and successful supervision, management, and organization of employees. Individual differences, motivation, morale, the organization of groups, the functioning of individuals in groups, and measurement are subjects of what has been called industrial or personnel psychology. With the emergence of engineering or human factors psychology as a special field, industrial and personnel psychology has come to be known somewhat inappropriately as industrial and organizational psychology. A more accurate name might be organizational—or perhaps organizational and personnel—psychology.

For nearly three generations, personnel psychologists have worked on the techniques used to select people for various types of jobs. They have concerned themselves with the development of interview and rating procedures and with tests that examine intelligence, aptitudes, interests, personality, and proficiency. It also is their responsibility to evaluate the effectiveness of these tests. The Army Alpha is the oldest known test of this type. The General Aptitude Test Battery and the various special batteries of the United States Employment Service are among the newer of the widely used personnel selection tests. However, most such tests are custom-built, that is, developed for use in a specific concern, and are kept confidential as part of its stock-in-trade as well as to keep the contents from being spoiled by becoming known to job applicants.

Some psychologists engaged in work of this type are measurement psychologists. But some in this field are personnel psychologists, that is, they are prepared for and engage in types of psychological work. Because of their demonstrated usefulness in employee selection, industrial and personnel psychologists have become involved in the development and evaluation of training methods of workers, as well as job analysis and evaluation. In addition, they conduct in-service training for employees, evaluate employees for promotion, ascertain the nature of effective supervision and leadership, study management communication methods, study the underlying factors that relate to good or poor employee morale, evaluate the effectiveness of methods and programs designed to improve morale, and, finally, relate such factors to production.

Organizational psychologists most frequently have a background in social psychology or have added that to their competencies in industrial psychology. They, too, work on problems of morale, leadership, and the organization of work. There has been considerable interest in recent years on worker participation in management or in management decisions having direct impact on them and their work. The solutions found by organizational psychologists are, understandably, more often in group functioning than they are in selection or training. There has, however, been a renewed interest in training and in counseling due in part to the rediscovery of such phenomena as "midcareer crises" and "burnout" and to acknowledge the importance of preparing for a good transition to retirement for our aging population.

To be effective in a business setting, the industrial psychologist must have a rather rare combination of qualities. In addition to being interested in research and psychology as a science, the industrial psychologist must be able to use psychological skills in practical situations. He or she must be able to communicate an understanding of a situation to people of widely varying backgrounds in order to win their confidence and thus establish effective working relationships with all levels in the organizational structure. These abilities require social and emotional maturity and a wide background of practical experience, particularly in the business world.

For these reasons, it is desirable that the potential organizational or personnel psychologist have had actual work experience in an industrial or business organization. This experience will give firsthand knowledge of the way an organization functions. However, personnel psychologists do go directly from undergraduate training to full-time doctoral programs; such programs should then include a supervised internship.

The education of organizational and personnel psychologists at the undergraduate level should, like that of other psychologists, be broad. It should include work in the social and biological sciences, education, and preferably a major in psychology. A background in business administration or engineering is helpful, but in such instances more supplementary graduate work is needed in the fields already mentioned. At the graduate level, it is possible to obtain technical competence in some personnel functions with one year of specialized training leading to the M.A. degree. Such training qualifies one as a personnel technician and stresses work in individual differences, the psychology of personality, statistics, testing, interviewing, and job analysis, with some study of labor economics and personnel administration.

More advanced educational preparation for work in personnel psychology, generally leading to a doctorate degree, involves studying the basic psychology courses. This is essential to a person who wants to qualify as a psychologist and is not possible in the brief technicians' training program. It is also important for the future organizational and personnel psychologist to study both basic and advanced courses in developmental psychology, the psychology of personality, social psychology, educational psychology, measurement, and group development. Various aspects of these fields are studied further in advanced courses in vocational, personnel, organizational, or industrial psychology. Some supplementary study of the sociology of industry, labor economics, and personnel management also is essential. While working toward a doctorate, it is highly desirable that the student experience a period of field work or internship. This experience is advantageous partly because it orients the student to a work situation and partly because it makes the problems being studied more meaningful.

Jobs for organizational and personnel psychologists are found in business and industry, in colleges and universities, in government and the armed forces, and in consulting firms. Many psychology professors in this specialty do consulting work, either as a part of their university work or independently. Some have consulting firms of their own. Noneducational employers of personnel psychologists are numerous.

The demand for highly trained organizational and personnel psychologists has continued because the problems of recession as well as growth require knowledgeable advice in making personnel and organizational changes. Positions for M.A.s have not been numerous, relatively speaking, but there has been sufficient demand to absorb most people qualified at this level. Many beginning jobs are filled by persons trained at the bachelor's level, but the competition for these jobs is great. Being placed in these jobs depends less on training than on practical experience, contacts, and personal characteristics. The outlook for this field is that there will continue to be a steady, even though reduced, demand for qualified men and women.

The American Board of Examiners in Psychology issues a Diploma in Industrial and Organizational Psychology to psychologists meeting its educational and experience requirements. These requirements include a doctorate, five years of appropriate experience, and passing written, oral, and practical examinations.

COUNSELING PSYCHOLOGY

Counseling psychology is the study of people as individuals, with the objective of helping them develop as fully as possible by making the best use of their abilities, interests, and opportunities. It is concerned with the development of principles, methods, and techniques that will be helpful in this work and in their application to people who might benefit from help in self-fulfillment. As an applied field, counseling psychology draws heavily on the basic fields of developmental, educational, personality, social, and metric psychology. It has much in common with personnel psychology on the one hand and with clinical on the other. It brings standard principles and techniques to bear on problems of understanding and helping individuals, and it supplements them with research on problems that are either peculiar to or highlighted in counseling.

Counseling psychologists interview high school and college students, employees, persons in need of vocational rehabilitation, and people in general who have problems concerning personal, social, educational, and vocational development and adjustment. In addition to the interview technique, they use tests and observational methods to collect additional information about their clients as individuals, in groups, and in the environments where they live and work. All of this is done to help their clients develop more fully and make better adjustment. They carry on research in the development and improvement of appraisal methods and counseling techniques. They study resources that may be helpful to their clients in improving social or vocational adjustments, and they may supervise the work of other counseling psychologists who are less experienced or less highly trained.

The training of counseling psychologists has been studied by committees of the professional association concerned with education below and through the doctorate. The counselor trained in psychology who specializes in vocational guidance should have at least two years of graduate training, although nonpsychologically trained school counselors now typically have one year of graduate preparation. However, training to the doctorate opens up a greater variety of higher level opportunities.

The undergraduate program should be broad, with work in the social and biological sciences including psychology and education. The counselor's graduate training should include work in developmental, educational, personality, social, and measurement psychology. It should also include courses designed to bring the principles of these fields to bear on problems of personal, marital, social, and vocational development and counseling. It should include some study of sociology, economics, the type of institutional setting in which the counselor will work, and particularly educational and occupational information and other resources helpful in counseling. There also should be training in the techniques of appraisal and counseling, with provision for some supervised experience in the use of these methods with clients. The American Board of Examiners in Psychology issues a Diploma in Counseling Psychology to psychologists with appropriate doctoral training and five years of experience who pass special written, oral, and practical examinations.

Doctoral education goes beyond the lower-level programs in providing the student with a better grounding in basic psychology, more advanced work in relevant psychological theory and counseling techniques, and particularly familiarity with and training in research that is essential to creative work in the field and to the progress of the profession. It covers a total of four years and includes a year of internship either on a full-time basis in the third year of graduate study or on a half-time basis during the last two years of graduate work.

Counseling psychologists and vocational counselors work in colleges and universities, usually in university counseling centers such as those at Minnesota, Ohio State, Illinois, Wisconsin, Iowa, Missouri, California, UCLA, and Stanford, often teaching as well as counseling. They are found in community guidance centers such as those in Cleveland, St. Louis, and New York; in employment bureaus and such social agencies such as the YMCA and the Jewish Welfare Agencies; in rehabilitation centers like New York's Institute for the Crippled and Disabled; in public and private hospitals; in the Veterans Administration; in the armed forces; and in a limited number of business and industrial organizations. A significant number are employed in consulting firms, sometimes to do counseling and sometimes to do executive evaluation work (the clinical study of persons in or being considered for key executive positions). An increasing number are in the full-time private practice of counseling psychology, partly because of the increasing recognition of the role that trained counselors can play in helping with situational problems relating to families, communities, and work and partly because the clinical competencies of those trained to the doctoral level lead to private practice in therapeutic counseling. When demand and interest result in such work, the distinction between counseling and clinical psychologists becomes difficult to make, despite counseling's emphasis on developmental and educational work as contrasted with remedial or reconstructive work.

Counseling psychology, combined with clinical and school psychology, makes up the largest percentage of doctoral level psychologists—70 percent.

The demand for the services of counseling psychologists has soared toward the end of each war (World War II, Korea, Vietnam, Persian

Gulf) with the increase of work needing to be done with returning servicemen and servicewomen, the shifting of war-industry workers, and the need to rehabilitate numbers of wounded and emotionally disturbed veterans. Former veterans' guidance centers generally were converted into permanent college or community counseling services, employing well-prepared counseling psychologists and vocational counselors. It was found in many situations that a staff composed of men and women trained at both the M.A. and Ph.D. or Ed.D. levels worked very effectively, setting a pattern now widespread in community colleges, four-year arts and engineering colleges, and universities.

Colleges and universities have employed counseling psychologists in other aspects of student personnel work, such as testing programs, discipline, mental health, student activities, and the direction of student services. Public school systems increasingly are seeking counseling psychologists with high school teaching experience as directors of guidance, and community guidance centers steadily have raised their standards and increased in number.

Antipoverty projects added new opportunities for leadership in the development of counseling and training programs and services. The budget cuts of the early 1980s reduced these community services and the professional opportunities associated with them, but there is still some continuing demand.

Counseling psychologists have taken on new roles in evaluating the employability of adults for the Social Security Administration and for Vocational Rehabilitation. The extension of insurance coverage, both governmental and private, to cover psychotherapy and, in some instances, vocational counseling designed to restore or to improve employability, also has opened new opportunities for counseling psychologists.

The Veterans Administration and the Rehabilitation Services Administration followed and assisted in these developments by raising standards, by supporting training programs in cooperation with a number of universities, and by employing a large number of well-trained counseling psychologists. Despite budget cuts, counseling psychology continues to offer opportunities in the services and programs of colleges, schools, community agencies, hospitals, and industries staffed by both M.A.s and Ph.D.s.

CLINICAL AND ABNORMAL PSYCHOLOGY

Clinical psychology is the study and treatment of emotionally disturbed or intellectually deficient individuals. The disturbance may be slight, as in normal development, or serious, as in psychoses. The deficiency may also be minor, as in some learning disabilities, or serious, as in severe mental retardation. These people are studied to determine their actual and potential levels of functioning (in terms of both accomplishment and happiness) and to help them make adjustments appropriate to their capacities and opportunities. Clinical psychology is the field of psychology most concerned with the development of principles, methods, and techniques to be applied to disturbed and handicapped people. In making these applications, clinical psychology draws heavily on the basic fields of abnormal, developmental, personality, social, and metric psychology together with neurology, physiology, genetics, and sociology. It synthesizes them in the study of emotional disturbance and mental deficiency and adds to the relevant store of knowledge and tools by conducting its own research on its own peculiar problems.

Abnormal psychology is the study of mental and emotional disorders. It is concerned with the development, manifestations, and treatment methods of personality deviations and intellectual defects, both organic and functional. It is an important part of the scientific basis of clinical psychology and psychiatry and contributes to the understanding of the normal personality.

Psychologists working in this field may study the relationships between the structure and nature of family relationships and the incidence of schizophrenia; specific language dysfunctions caused by different loci of brain injury; and the differences in the responses of various types of disturbed individuals (for example, schizophrenics and brain damage cases) to psychological tests. These are also the research activities of clinical psychologists; most persons conducting research in or devoting most of their time to teaching abnormal psychology are clinical psychologists. There are a few exceptions, particularly experimental or physiological psychologists or students of personality, who have directed their research activities into this area and who make a special contribution through the use of concepts and methods most highly developed in their fields.

A clinical psychologist interviews a patient to get an understanding of the patient's background and status, or the psychologist may rely on case reports if the patient is too disturbed, young, or deficient to be interviewed. Clinical psychologists may interview relatives or associates to see the patient as others do. They administer tests to obtain a more objective and well-rounded picture of the patient and write diagnostic reports concerning the patient. They may discuss the patient with psychiatrists, social workers, pediatricians, judges, and other specialists who refer cases for diagnostic study or with whom they work in a team relationship. They may consult with parents, teachers, or physicians. They may counsel the patient, provide psychotherapy, or refer the patient to another type of service. They may supervise other psychologists with less experience and training. They may conduct research in psychodiagnosis and psychotherapy and teach related courses.

Standards for the doctoral training of clinical psychologists were established in 1947 by a committee of the American Psychological Association and have been reaffirmed since then by its Education and Training Board. Undergraduate recommendations by the APA include psychology, biological and physical sciences, mathematics and statistics, education, social sciences, history of culture, psychology as revealed in literature, and languages. The objective is not to specify courses and credits but to ensure a broad liberal education with work in certain areas necessary for graduate work in psychology.

In graduate training, the objective in most universities is to produce a psychologist who is acquainted with the basic areas of psychological theory, research, and methods. This should embrace such subjects as general psychology (physiological and comparative, history and schools of psychology, developmental psychology and psychopathology), diagnostic methods, therapy, research methods, and related disciplines (physiology, related medical information, social organization and social pathology, and cultural anthropology). In a few programs, there is less emphasis on general psychology and research, with the objective of preparing practitioners. The program may take four years and includes a full-time internship during the third year or a half-time internship during both the third and fourth years.

There has been much discussion of the need for standards in the training of clinical technicians below the doctoral level. Some colleges and universities offer an M.A. in clinical psychology. Unlike the field of counseling psychology, however, clinical psychology has as yet reached no agreement to standardize such programs, much less their content. The American Board of Examiners in Psychology issues a Diploma in Clinical Psychology to highly qualified clinicians comparable to those given in industrial and counseling psychology.

Another important trend in the development of clinical psychology—arising from interest in practicing rather than in doing research and a sometimes associated belief that research training is irrelevant to or interferes with training in psychodiagnostics and psychotherapy—has been the development of schools of professional psychology (meaning clinical, generally disregarding counseling, industrial and organizational, engineering, and school psychology). These have grown up largely on the West Coast but a few also have started on the East Coast. They give a practitioners' degree, usually the Psy.D. For admission they adhere to the usual undergraduate degree with an emphasis on psychology, but they are generally less influenced by traditional standards than are the graduate schools of the stronger universities.

As a result of the emphasis on doctoral education and the uncertain status of subdoctoral training in clinical psychology, the best positions in this field tend to be open only to people with the doctorate. Clinical psychologists with the Ph.D., Psy.D., or Ed.D. are employed in universities accredited for graduate training in this field and in other colleges and universities as instructors in this specialty. They also work in university clinics, medical schools, and hospitals as clinicians and research workers. They are employed in the Veterans Administration, the United States Public Health Service, and the armed forces.

Many also work in institutions for the delinquent or mentally defective, in prisons, in public and private hospitals, in mental health or child guidance clinics, and in psychological clinics sponsored by community organizations. Others are employed in consulting firms doing executive evaluation (clinical personnel) work. Finally, there are many in private practice (more than one-third). Some of these work in cooperation with other practitioners, such as psychiatrists, pediatricians, and social workers; others work independently. Clinical psychologists without the doctorate are most generally employed in junior staff positions or in institutions that are unable to compete for fully qualified clinicians.

The demand for clinical psychologists increased beyond all precedent or expectation toward the end of World War II and surged again after other major military efforts. This increase is partly because of the great volume of work to be done with emotionally inadequate or disturbed members of the service and partly because of an increased public awareness of the importance of human resources and human adjustment. In order to meet this need, large-scale programs were set up by the Veterans Administration and the United States Public Health Service after World War II and a smaller program by the army for the training of clinical psychologists at the doctoral level. Furthermore, the American Psychological Association assumed the responsibility of evaluating and accrediting graduate training in clinical psychology, a move that has since been expanded to include concern for psychological training in all applied areas. Actual accrediting is done only when requested by outside fund-granting agencies for such fields as clinical, counseling, and school psychology, and upon request of the university.

SCHOOL PSYCHOLOGY

School psychologists often have functioned as clinical psychologists in an educational setting. They are concerned with problems of adjustment, mental health, and school achievement, primarily in elementary schools. School psychology has therefore drawn on the basic fields of developmental, personality, social, and metric psychology together with physiology, sociology, social work, educational psychology, and educational philosophy. It makes its own synthesis of these other fields to understand children who have problems adjusting to school. It endeavors to help them directly as well as through their parents and teachers to make better adjustments and get the most from their educational opportunities. In the process, school psychologists conduct research to make better applications of their techniques and to provide themselves with more effective working tools.

More than ever before, school psychologists have a broad responsibility for the educational adjustment and mental health of students. They work with teachers, administrators, and parents to develop healthy emotional and effective learning experiences for children. School psychologists may work with a group of teachers on a problem such as the psychological factors involved in the poor scholastic achievement of bright children. They also may work as members of teams in clarifying procedures related to the classification of pupils, the development of a desirable program for induction of children into kindergarten, a survey of progress in particular fields of academic achievement, or the evaluation of a new program. Intensive study is made into any troublesome area involving a student's personal development when requested by the principal, teacher, or supervisor.

School psychologists also administer group and individual tests to schoolchildren to ascertain their intellectual and proficiency levels and to locate areas in which they need special help. They interview children and may conduct play therapy with them for diagnostic purposes. They interview parents and teachers to round out their pictures of the children. They also may observe the children in work and play situations. They write up diagnostic reports and case studies in special instances and then discuss these with other specialists at child guidance clinics, at health centers, or in staff conferences in the school.

School psychologists generally refer those children who require psychotherapy to other agencies, although in some instances they may conduct it themselves. In addition, they may do some parent counseling. Increasingly, school psychologists work through classroom teachers to bring about better adjusted children. In addition, school psychologists may supervise remedial teaching or special classroom work for slow learners or handicapped children. More and more, they act as staff consultants and contribute to the study and solution of curricular and instructional problems that involve psychological understanding or techniques.

The principal emphasis in the education of school psychologists today is on working effectively with teachers and helping them improve their handling of children's problems. Increasingly, school psychologists are expected to assume leadership in helping teachers, administrators, and curriculum workers develop programs in accordance with sound learning and developmental principles and to be a force in helping the community understand and accept needed school changes.

The education of most school psychologists, like that of many clinical psychologists and most vocational counselors, until recently has ended at the master's degree level. As in other specialties, however, the need for higher standards has become evident. Therefore, an increasing number of school psychologists are earning doctoral degrees. When the school psychologist was little more than a mental and educational tester, a year of preparation seemed sufficient. Now, however, the school psychologist plays a more important role in education as a diagnostician, therapist, supervisor of child development and remedial education, curriculum consultant, and participant in the program of in-service education for teachers. The importance of more advanced training is obvious, and the demand for more highly trained people is greater.

The American Psychological Association's Education and Training Board and its Division of School Psychologists, with financial aid from the United States Public Health Service, have studied educational standards in this field. They recommended two preparatory programs for people who wish to become school psychologists. The first is a two-year training program, open only to teachers who have taught in elementary or secondary schools. The other is a three-year doctoral program. On the undergraduate level, work in education is preferred. On the graduate level, the work should stress developmental, educational, personality, social, and measurement psychology with supporting work in physiology, sociology, and education. In addition, there should be intensive work in the diagnostic and therapeutic techniques involved in this area of psychology. This in turn should be supplemented by supervised practice in individual work with children in schools and clinics and in consulting with teachers and school administrators. The advantage of doctoral work is that it permits the inclusion of more work in diagnostic and treatment techniques, personality theory, research, and practical experience.

While most school psychologists have a doctorate, a larger number of school psychologists have training only at the master's level. Like educational psychology, school psychology has traditionally attracted many women; unlike it, it employs many M.A.s. This may become less true as consulting and program evaluation roles expand.

School psychologists work in public and private schools and occasionally in school psychological clinics. Usually, however, especially in the case of public schools, they work at the board of education of a particular school district, making visits to individual schools. Those with doctoral training frequently transfer to teaching positions in colleges and universities.

Those who remain with a board of education may advance to director of guidance or supervisor of psychological services for a school system. This is particularly true of those school psychologists whose education and experience have given them training in counseling psychology and those who have worked with adolescents. School psychologists who have had extensive experience with exceptional children often will advance to administrative positions in special education programs.

If employed by a public school system, school psychologists must be certified in the state in which they work. The requirements for certification vary from state to state. They can, however, usually be met in one year of properly planned graduate work. Students should check the requirements of the states in which they expect to be employed. A program of study should be planned with these requirements in mind. There is no specialty certification in this field by professional associations.

The demand for well-trained and effective school psychologists is considerable. The development of special programs for disadvantaged and special needs children highlights this need.

SPORTS PSYCHOLOGY

Sports psychologists are concerned with the psychological stimuli that affect and improve athletic performance. They also look at the effects of exercise and physical activity on psychological adjustment and health. Sports psychologists typically work in academic settings and/or as consultants for sports teams. They often work in conjunction with sports medicine professionals.

EMERGING SPECIALTIES, RELATED FIELDS, AND INTERDISCIPLINARY BRIDGES

As the specialties of psychology mature and branch out to meet new challenges, several new centers of interests—emerging specialties, really—have developed. Most of these involve building bridges to other disciplines, usually around applied issues. One of the most attractive at present is health psychology, a field that combines aspects of physiological, social, counseling, and clinical psychology. Health psychologists, who may be either practitioners or researchers, focus their work on the role of psychological functioning in the promotion of health and the prevention and treatment of illness. Thus their research or applied work may focus on the origins or treatment of obesity, smoking, and cardiovascular disease, or on the management of stress and adherence to a prescribed program of medication and exercise. Doctoral programs in health psychology have started at a number of universities, and their continued growth is widely anticipated in light of scientific progress and available research funds.

Somewhat related is pediatric psychology. In this field, clinical and developmental psychologists conduct research on aspects of medical practice that are unique to children, such as the optimal policy on a parent staying overnight in a hospital with a young patient, or how to help a child with leukemia adapt to the difficult medical regimen and the massive disruption of daily life. Pediatric psychologists who actively work with patients are initially trained as clinicians, and they have taken additional practical or internship training to specialize.

Another specialty is family psychology, which is concerned with the understanding and improvement of family dynamics and individual development within the family. Again, both research and applied issues dominate discussion in this field, and family psychologists might be primarily researchers or clinicians trained in family therapy.

Forensic psychology is another rapidly growing area of specialization. It consists of the theoretical and applied study of psychology and the law in such areas as investigating the mental competence to stand trial of persons accused of criminal acts, assessing neuropsychological damage of persons involved in accidents, and evaluating the relative strengths and weaknesses of two divorcing parents who each want custody of a child. Specialization in psychology and the law is usually achieved within another, more traditional program (such as clinical or social psychology), often with postdoctoral training.

Cross-cultural psychology is a focus for some psychologists. Some of the impetus for this comes from a theoretical appreciation of culture as an organizing context for the development and regulation of behavior, and some from the increasing international communication of psychologists around the world. What was in the 1950s a near monopoly by American scientists has now become global in its application and activity, and cross-cultural psychology attempts to understand the diversity of results around the world—indeed within many countries, such as the United States—and use this perspective to improve our theories of human behavior. There are at present no doctoral programs in cross-cultural psychology, and the specialty is usually achieved in conjunction with a more traditional field such as social or developmental psychology.

In all of these areas, psychologists find themselves working with and drawing on the literature of colleagues in anthropology, law, medicine, biology, and other related fields. Innovations in these fields are often exciting and productive, and some are attracting significant research funds. They are some of the most rapidly growing areas and among the most appealing to students.

CHAPTER 3

PROSPECTS IN PSYCHOLOGY

According to the Bureau of Labor Statistics, employment of psychologists is expected to grow about as fast as the average for all occupations through 2008. Employment in health care will grow fastest in outpatient mental health and substance abuse treatment clinics. Job opportunities also will arise in schools, public and private social service agencies, and management consulting services.

Companies will use psychologists' expertise in survey design, analysis, and research to provide marketing evaluation and statistical analysis. The increase in employee assistance programs, which offer employees help with personal problems, should also spur job growth.

Opportunities for people holding doctorates from leading universities in areas with an applied emphasis, such as clinical, counseling, health, and educational psychology, should have particularly good prospects. Psychologists with extensive training in quantitative research methods and computer science may have a competitive edge over applicants without this background.

MASTER'S DEGREE HOLDERS

Graduates with a master's degree in psychology qualify for positions in school and industrial-organizational psychology. Graduates of master's degree programs in school psychology should have the best job prospects, because schools are expected to increase student counseling and mental health services.

Master's degree holders with several years of industrial experience can obtain jobs in consulting and marketing research. Other master's degree holders may find jobs as psychological assistants in the community mental health field, which often requires direct supervision by a licensed psychologist. Still others may find jobs involving research and data collection and analysis in universities, government, or private companies.

BACHELOR'S DEGREE HOLDERS

As is expected, very few opportunities directly related to psychology will exist for bachelor's degree holders. Some may find jobs as assistants in rehabilitation centers, or in other jobs involving data collection and analysis. Those who meet state certification requirements may become high school psychology teachers.

RAPID GROWTH

The great majority of American psychologists belong to the American Psychological Association (APA), although there still are many persons trained or functioning as psychologists who do not belong to their major professional association. The growth of this professional association parallels the growth of the field. In 1920, there were approximately 400 APA members; in 1940, there were about 2,500; in 1950, the number was approximately 7,500; in 1960, they numbered some 18,000; in 1975, about 40,000; and now there are more than 159,000 members. The increase in the number of psychologists was slow and steady from 1900 to 1920, somewhat more rapid from 1920 to 1940, and extremely rapid after 1945. It still increases, as psychology continues to be one of the most popular undergraduate and graduate fields of study.

The mere fact of increase in the number of psychologists is important, but not sufficient for someone considering the opportunities in the field. The next question is, what are they doing? What proportion of them are employed, and where are they employed? How much do they earn?

One outcome of the recent rapid growth of psychology is of passing interest: it is a profession of relatively young men and women. The stereotype of the gray-bearded professor practitioner is no longer, if it ever was, justified. Nearly one-third of the members of the American Psychological Association are less than forty years of age, and most psychologists have earned their doctorates during the past twenty years.

**Primary Full-time Employment Settings
of Doctorate Recipients in Psychology: 1997**

Data on Education and Employment—Doctoral

The largest single proportion of new doctorates was located in human service settings (hospitals and clinics, etc.) followed by higher education. The business and industry setting here does not include those in private or group practices.

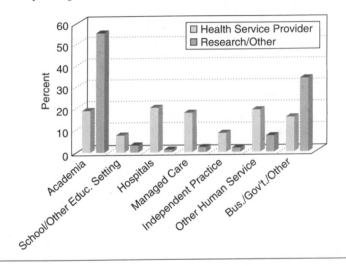

Reprinted with permission from the APA.

WHERE PSYCHOLOGISTS WORK

Colleges and universities employ about 35 to 40 percent of America's doctoral psychologists. This percentage was lower during the postwar expansion of applied psychology, and then increased, peaking in the early 1970s. It has declined during past years as shrinking university and college enrollments lead to static or reduced faculties and as more psychologists seek or make employment elsewhere. The academic psychologists of today, unlike those of a generation or two ago, devote more time to research and to practice than did their precursors. More than one-fourth of them also do some outside consulting work. Psychologists typically work about forty-five hours per week, and more than one-fifth work over fifty-five hours per week. There is moonlighting in psychology, as in other fields, and professors, more than those in most fields, carry their work over into their free time, not only for remuneration, but also out of sheer interest, as shown in a number of studies of the personalities of psychologists and other academics.

Private practice in clinical psychology on a full-time basis is the second largest employment setting for doctoral psychologists. This is a considerable increase in numbers during the past decade. There are currently far more professional psychologists in private practice in large cities, such as New York, Chicago, and Los Angeles, than ever before. Apparently, the general increase in the demand for psychological services, along with changes in the opportunities for insurance reimbursement, has resulted in an increased demand for private consultation services. This, in turn, has resulted in an increased interest on the part of psychologists to meet this demand. This need is also being met in part by academically employed psychologists who have a part-time clinical practice.

Hospitals and clinics employ about 30 percent of doctoral psychologists. The demand for clinical and counseling psychologists has been so great during the last generation that the Veterans Administration, the United States Public Health Service, and the United States Army have long subsidized the doctoral education of about five hundred psychologists each year. The numbers and financial resources of such arrangements have declined in recent years; however, some do continue, and the needs of federal agencies merely reflect the continuing general demand for people in clinical and counseling psychology in other types of hospitals, clinics, educational institutions, and social agencies as well as business and industry.

Responses to the health care crisis that became a major focus of policy debate in the early 1990s will have a significant effect on psychologists in private practice and in hospitals and clinics. Under programs of managed care, such as health maintenance organizations and preferred provider organizations, there is a financial incentive for preventive care and early intervention. Psychologists have a central role in the mental health aspect of managed care, and they are often involved in evaluation and utilization studies as well, in which scientists and administrators track and analyze how patients use the services that are offered and whether these services are as efficient and effective as possible. Although there are a number of issues to be resolved as new organizations and new roles are worked out, it appears that the private practitioner model will become more rare in the future, with a much larger number of psychologists working in, or affiliated with, networks of managed care.

Public schools and other nonprofit organizations employ another 67 percent of doctoral psychologists. Programs for the preparation of school psychologists now receive federal subsidies, as do clinical and counseling programs. Despite the surpluses of graduates in most teaching fields and the pressures on school budgets, specialties such as this still thrive, especially when they include competence in dealing with learning disabilities and high level consultant skills.

Business and industry employ about 20 percent of doctoral level psychologists. Between 1973 and 1997 the decline in the proportion of psychologists in academic settings and the increase in business/industry were the result of a large increase in psychologists in the health service provider subfields (clinical, counseling, school), coupled with increasing opportunities for work in for-profit and business settings.

Government agencies also employ about 10 percent of America's doctoral psychologists. Psychologists are employed in agencies such as civil service commissions, employment services, and departments of education. Openings of this type had been numerous until recent cutbacks, but even now there is a demand in some areas; advertisements in the American Psychological Association's *APA Monitor* evidence this fact.

Federal and state support of educational research, development, and demonstration work has increased the size and number of organizations—both governmental and nonprofit—employing specialists (M. A. and doctoral) in developmental, educational, measurement, and social psychology.

Statistics vary depending on the source and factors studied. The previous numbers were based on APA findings in 1997. The *Occupational Outlook Handbook,* complied by the Bureau of Labor Statistics, offers these 1998 figures—the most recent available:

Psychologists held about 166,000 jobs in 1998. Educational institutions employed about four out of ten salaried psychologists in positions other than teaching, such as counseling, testing, research, and administration. Three out of ten were employed in health services, primarily in hospitals, mental health clinics, rehabilitation centers, nursing homes, and other health facilities.

Government agencies at the federal, state, and local levels employed about 17 percent. Governments employ psychologists in hospitals, clinics, correctional facilities, and other settings. The Department of Veterans Affairs and the Department of Defense employ a majority of the psychologists working for federal agencies.

GEOGRAPHIC DISTRIBUTION

While discussing the number of psychologists, it may be helpful to add a few words about their geographic distribution. As a relatively new science and profession, psychology is more in demand in the highly developed parts of the country than in those areas that are less advanced economically and technologically. Psychologists tend to be found largely in the centers of population, and particularly in cities in the Northeast, the Midwest, and the Pacific Coast. New York and California lead with about 11 percent of the country's psychologists each, Pennsylvania and Texas are next, while Alaska, North Dakota, Wyoming, and Delaware have the fewest psychologists. Of course the population as a whole has a somewhat similar distribution across the country, but there are still considerable geographic differences in the ratio of psychologists to the general population.

WOMEN AND MINORITIES IN PSYCHOLOGY

A 1999 APA survey shows that 49.1 percent of psychologists are women. This is a huge gain in the last decade. A 1991 survey showed that only 35 percent of psychologists were women. But in spite of this gain, there is still a long way to go.

Women typically hold lower ranks in universities and colleges. Another 1999 APA survey reveals that 70 percent of male psychologists on the faculty of universities and colleges are tenured. That means that only 30 percent of tenured faculty are women, yet women represent approximately half the faculty on the tenure track as well as nontenure track faculty.

Of the top two ranks, approximately 75 percent of full professors are men; and approximately 58 percent of associate professors are men. Women make a few strides at the assistant level position, at 52 percent, and are in the majority—approximately 65 percent—at the lowest level of lecturer.

In general, women also hold lower ranking positions in other settings. In the practice of clinical psychology, most clients are women, but most clinical psychologists are men.

Ethnic minorities have been minorities indeed in psychology. APA membership in 1991 included 1,353 members of Hispanic origin; 1,173 African-Americans; 890 Asian Americans; and 332 Native Americans. In 1991 about 75 percent of APA members were non-Hispanic Caucasian, a disproportionate number, but a situation typical of the scientific community and many other professions.

In 1999 the APA member demographics show some improvement. Of the 159,000 APA members, 83,186 responded to the survey. Of those, 366 are Native Americans; 1,178 are Asian; 1,605 are Hispanic; 1,322 are African-American; 434 list themselves as "other"; and 59,133 are non-Hispanic Caucasian—71.1 percent.

Other surveys show a steady growth of new doctorates awarded to women and minorities. One consequence of the increase in women and minority psychologists is the new perspectives lent to the field and APA's desire to be responsive to new interest areas. They have established new divisions within APA, new committees, and new boards. Many university programs also have been established with the aim of attracting women and minorities to psychology.

CHAPTER 4

THE REWARDS OF PSYCHOLOGY

The rewards of psychology are both tangible and intangible. Tangible rewards include earnings and the fringe benefits that go with them, such as housing, medical care, and retirement provisions. Intangible rewards include the satisfaction that comes with doing something that one likes, considers important, and that others value. Psychological studies of job satisfaction and morale have amply demonstrated the importance of both types of rewards.

FINANCIAL REWARDS

In 1999 the APA conducted extensive salary surveys among its doctoral-level members. The salary range is wide and varies depending upon work setting and number of years' experience. The new graduate working a nine-month contract at the bottom of the university hierarchy might start out at $32,000. At the top of the ladder salaries exceed $70,000; university researchers earn close to $100,000, and those in business and industry well over $100,000.

In general, salaries in the field of psychology compare well with those for chemists and engineers and are superior to those of social workers and teachers. Financially, psychologists are in the top 10 percent of the employed population.

Recent salary levels for doctoral-level psychologists working in different settings with different levels of experience are summarized in Table 1, and salary levels for master's degree holders in Table 2.

Table 1:   1999—Average Salaries of Doctoral-Level Psychologists in Various Positions

Position	Annual Average Salary
ACADEMIC FACULTY	
Assistant Professor	$40,757
Associate Professor	53,060
Full Professor	76,178
RESEARCH POSITIONS	
Private Research	
2–4 years	$58,143
5–9 years	58,500
15–19 years	86,333
University Psychology Dept.	
2–4 years	$28,429
University Research Center	
2–4 years	46,429
10–14 years	60,500
Government Research	
20–24 years	81,400
DIRECT HUMAN SERVICES—CLINICAL PSYCHOLOGY	
Elementary/Secondary	
20–24 years	$87,000
Public General Hospital	
5–9 years	56,400
Private General Hospital	
5–9 years	59,917
10–14 years	72,000
VA Hospital	
5–9 years	61,111
Individual Private Practice	
2–4 years	$75,600
10–14 years	83,711
20–24 years	89,282
DIRECT HUMAN SERVICES—COUNSELING PSYCHOLOGY	
University/College Counseling Center	
5–9 years	$45,500
10–14 years	51,357
25–29 years	62,889

VA Hospital
5–9 years   60,000
Individual Private Practice
2–4 years   49,833
10–14 years   56,750
20–24 years   81,673

DIRECT HUMAN SERVICES—SCHOOL PSYCHOLOGY
Elementary/Secondary School
5–9 years $53,857
10–14 years   66,800
School System District Office
20–24 years   60,667
Individual Private Practice
10–14 years   79,400
20–24 years   122,200

ADMINISTRATION OF HUMAN SERVICES
University/College Counseling Center
2–4 years $42,333
5–9 years   58,111
10–14 years   58,444
Public General Hospital
15–19 years   72,750
Business/Industry
15–19 years   141,800
25–29 years   122,500
Nonprofit Organization
10–14 years   79,500

APPLIED PSYCHOLOGY—INDUSTRIAL/ORGANIZATIONAL
Consulting Firm
2–4 years $59,111
5–9 years   101,222
15–19 years   109,000
20–24 years   180,200
Business/Industry
2–4 years   70,200
5–9 years   84,000
15–19 years   123,167

**Table 2:   1999—Average Salaries of Master's-Level Psychologists
in Various Positions**

Position	*Annual Average Salary*
ACADEMIC FACULTY	
University Psychology Department	
Assistant Professor	$36,000
Two-Year College	
Full Professor	$49,889
DIRECT HUMAN SERVICES—CLINICAL PSYCHOLOGY	
Individual Private Practice	
10–14 years	$74,000
15–19 years	52,857
Criminal Justice System	
5–9 years	$44,200
DIRECT HUMAN SERVICES—COUNSELING PSYCHOLOGY	
Individual Private Practice	
5–9 years	$46,000
10–14 years	47,800
DIRECT HUMAN SERVICES—SCHOOL PSYCHOLOGY	
Elementary/Secondary	
2–4 years	$41,200
15–19 years	61,400
APPLIED PSYCHOLOGY—INDUSTRIAL/ORGANIZATIONAL	
Consulting Firm	
2–4 years	$52,000
5–9 years	73,692

In 1999 doctoral-level psychologists who worked in business and industry, whether for a corporation or self-employed as a consultant, were the best paid, along with clinical psychologists in private practice. The lowest paid were master's degree holders working in academic institutions. Ph.D.s also were paid the least in academic institutions.

What all these figures add up to is simply this: Psychologists, especially those with the doctorate degree, make as good a living as most other professional men and women. Despite differences between their pay and that of some other professional groups, despite salary differences depending on where they work and what their specialties are, psychologists earn enough to lead interesting lives and to raise their families according to good standards. Few acquire wealth, but few suffer hardship. Moreover, what they do is useful to society.

Material rewards for psychologists vary with the type of organization. In private practice or consulting work, psychologists obviously must provide themselves with retirement benefits, medical care, housing, and the like. They also will receive social security benefits after retirement. At the other extreme, psychologists commissioned in one of the armed forces have the benefits of medical care, retirement, housing, and commissary facilities traditionally available to military personnel. Colleges, hospitals, social agencies, school systems, and business and industry fall somewhere in between as to the type and number of benefits they provide. With respect to the nonsalary rewards, psychologists are just like physicians, engineers, lawyers, machinists, truck drivers, and janitors; what they receive depends on where they work.

INTANGIBLE REWARDS

Now let us look at the intangible rewards, the work satisfactions, and the way of life that a psychologist enjoys. These fall into a twofold classification: those that are associated with being a psychologist and those that are associated with working in institutions and organizations where psychologists are employed. Let us look at the former first, since it is more peculiar to psychology.

The work satisfactions of psychologists come from the application of scientific methods to the understanding of human behavior and to the solution of problems of human relations and personal adjustment. Psychologists' work combines in a unique way the methods of science and the subject matter of human relations. They are in a position to obtain the intellectual satisfactions of discovery, understanding, and invention at the same time that they experience the emotional satisfaction of working with and for people. Depending on the field of specialization, psychologists can emphasize or minimize the extent to which they do any one of these.

An experimental psychologist may have relatively brief and transient contacts with people in the course of work, and the helping of people may be very indirect. However, the experimental psychologist's intellectual satisfaction in understanding the principles of behavior, the development of theory, and the design of experiments and equipment may be great.

Clinical or counseling psychologists may combine the intellectual satisfaction of understanding the behavior of individuals and of exploring the many partially understood aspects of personality. They have the emotional satisfaction of helping people function more effectively and achieve self-fulfillment.

The research psychologist in a large organization, whether educational, industrial, military, or health, has the intellectual satisfaction derived from applying experimental methods to problems of the development and use of human resources. This is combined with the emotional satisfaction of making the people with whom he or she works more effective, thus contributing to the strength of our country's educational systems, economy, welfare, or defense.

The instructor in a college or university combines the intellectual satisfaction of organizing, sharing with others, and perhaps adding to the store of knowledge concerning human behavior, along with the emotional satisfaction of working with students and guiding their growth and early professional development.

Interviewing workers, teaching classes, planning statistical analyses, designing learning experiments, interpreting personality tests, reading research reports, writing texts, watching rats in a maze, teasing out the meanings of a variety of case materials, observing the behavior of children in play—these and the myriad other things psychologists do are time-consuming, often slow, sometimes tedious, rarely easy; but for many persons these can be thrilling activities.

To think up a neat and convincing design for an experiment that will put some theory to the test; to find the underlying trends that make the seemingly discordant elements of a client's personality form a meaningful whole; to help a patient or client develop more effective behavior patterns or find better outlets for his or her talents; to organize the findings of a number of discrete research studies into a chapter in a book that makes useful to others a new principle or an important diagnostic technique; to share with others the results of new research that has been well conceived and executed—these are deeply satisfying activities in which psychologists engage. They are exciting events when they happen, and they do not pall with age and experience. If anything, time makes them more enjoyable and more rewarding.

Psychologists enjoy a comfortable lifestyle. They may not have a wealth of material things, but neither do they suffer any hardship. Psychologists do not stand at the top of the social prestige ladder, but they are high enough to be respected by all and low enough to be acceptable to most. Their work brings them in contact with other educated persons with whom they can share the intellectual and aesthetic interests that usually develop during the course of college and graduate education. The psychologist's income is sufficient to indulge these interests, share them with neighbors, and rear children to appreciate and enjoy them.

SOME DISADVANTAGES

Along with the advantages, the disadvantages of being a psychologist should be commented on here. But whenever these terms are used, one must ask, "advantages and disadvantages for whom?" It is an old saying that one person's meat is another person's poison. Each reader of such a book as this must ask whether the type of work and the way of life described is appealing, whether it will enable the attainment of valued goals, and whether it will provide the opportunity to be the kind of person one would like to be. The young man or woman who is more interested in the things that money will buy than in the things done to earn the money will find some disadvantages in psychology as a profession. While we have seen that psychologists earn as much as most professional groups, they earn less than people in other fields such as medicine and the higher levels of business, and the work is intellectually and often emotionally demanding.

The young woman or man who enters psychology will find that there are certain drawbacks associated with the type of institution or enterprise in which she or he works. In an educational institution, the psychologist probably will have too little clerical assistance. In a mental hospital or school for the mentally retarded, social life will probably be rather limited, for there is a tendency for staff members of such an institution to live on or near the isolated grounds and to become a little community of their own.

In a business organization, the young psychologist will lead a life like that of an office clerk if he or she is employed at the technician level, and like that of an executive if employed in a position of leadership. In the former case, the psychologist may feel like an insignificant cog in a big machine. In the latter instance, he or she may find it necessary to keep up with the Joneses, buying more expensive clothes and generally engaging in the socially competitive activities of the "status seekers." As a behavioral scientist, the psychologist is likely to consider such competition superficial and perhaps unhealthy, although some view it simply as a game one plays.

The work satisfactions and way of life associated with working in the organizations where psychologists find employment are not peculiar to the field. Psychologists who work in schools share the satisfactions, problems, and the way of life of teachers. Those who work in hospitals share satisfactions and problems similar to those of physicians, nurses, occupational therapists, and others who also work there. Psychologists who work in colleges or graduate schools share the work satisfactions and living conditions common to college professors. Those who work in business in many ways resemble businessmen and businesswomen, for they share their work and their social lives, even while maintaining a professional identity.

In choosing the type of organization in which to work, the psychologist also chooses the type of community in which to live, the friends with whom to associate, the kind of home to have, and the children with whom his or her children will grow up and go to school.

WHO SHOULD ENTER PSYCHOLOGY?

So far we have seen something of the status and prospects of the field of psychology and something of the nature of the psychologist's work. In the next chapter, we shall look further into the field of psychology, examining its special branches before taking up the subject of the psychologist's education and training. First, however, let us take a moment to ask what sort of person should enter this field.

To be fully trained as a psychologist, one must have a doctorate, and to be employable as a technician in psychology, a master's degree is highly desirable. This means that a young man or woman considering the field should have at least enough academic ability to be capable of graduate study at a university. If one aspires to a position of leadership, one should be capable of the advanced study and research necessary for a Ph.D., Psy.D., or Ed.D. degree.

Psychology is a scientific profession devoted to the study of human behavior and the improvement of human adjustment. This means that the student of psychology should be a person who believes that knowledge is important, that time and energy should be spent in finding out what is true, and that principles and facts should be put to work in the interest of human welfare. It means that the student should consider knowledge and welfare ultimately more important than one's own material well-being, prestige, or aesthetic values, although these, too, have their proper place in one's life.

Psychology involves careful and precise work with large numbers of detailed observations concerning human or animal behavior, bringing together and understanding these data by statistical or other methods, reading widely and deeply in theoretical and applied subjects, and dealing with people as colleagues, clients, subjects, and students. The extent to which a given psychologist does each of these things depends partly on his or her specialty and partly on the kind of institution or organization in which he or she carries on the work of his or her special field.

But all psychologists need to be interested in the careful study of behavior and in collecting, organizing, and understanding data on behavior. All need scholarly interests and work habits. Interest in working with people may vary considerably, for in some specialties the psychologist may deal only indirectly with people other than professional colleagues or students. In other specialties the psychologist works closely with people of varied backgrounds and personal characteristics.

The personality requirements of psychology are to some extent suggested by the interest requirements. Psychologists need patience and persistence in working with varied and complex data, coupled with the ability to work toward remote goals that are difficult to attain. If they are employed in the applied or professional specialties, they need to be tolerant of individual differences and personality deviations in others. In clinical, counseling, and especially school psychology, a wholesome personal adjustment and a genuine acceptance of and interest in others are crucial.

As a social science that has contributed greatly to the understanding of bias and prejudice, psychology is an occupation that is relatively free of bias as to sex, race, religion, or physical handicap. Female psychologists, for example, occupy a number of important positions in psychology, including president of the national American Psychological Association, although proportionately fewer than their share. This may be true because they have done proportionately less research and writing, are less favored for administrative positions (particularly in business), and travel less. These differences are themselves influenced by sex-role stereotyping, which many organizations and individuals are actively working to change. In psychology, women have experienced less bias than in most professions, and recognition generally has been given readily and freely to anyone who has earned it. In the past, discrimination against African-Americans and Hispanics has gone unnoticed, but here, too, corrective steps have been taken.

CHAPTER 5

EDUCATION AND TRAINING

During the twentieth century, preparation for employment in a profession had become increasingly a matter of graduate study. First medicine and dentistry, then law and social work shifted their professional training from the undergraduate to the graduate level. College teaching long has required from one to three years of graduate preparation. The professions that do not require graduate preparation have been raising their standards in such ways as to suggest that graduate study will soon be a requirement. For example, high school teachers in some states are now required to include a year of graduate study in their preparation; engineering schools increasingly require five years of preparation, of which the first two are in the liberal arts; and architecture in some universities is an undergraduate program, in others a mixture of undergraduate and graduate study, and in still others (including some of the most distinguished), exclusively a graduate offering.

As a profession that was long dominated by college teachers, psychology since its beginnings has shared in the tradition and practice of graduate education. As increasing numbers of psychologists became engaged in applying psychological principles and methods in institutions and enterprises other than colleges, the tradition of graduate preparation was reinforced by the need for breadth of understanding combined with mastery of a substantial body of technical knowledge. Thus psychologists employed in medical settings found that if their special skills and instruments were to be used effectively, they themselves had to be more than technicians. They had to be professional workers with the depth and breadth of understanding of psychology, behavior, and physiology that enabled them to work with physicians as their peers.

Psychologists working in schools and colleges in nonteaching capacities found that if they were to make a contribution to education, they had to be more than measurement specialists. They had to be students of people and of society with a broad understanding of educational problems and processes. Psychologists engaged in the application of psychology to business and industry found that they, too, had to be more than technicians. It was necessary for them to be scientific and professional workers with considerable training if they were to have any success in putting psychology to work.

UNDERGRADUATE EDUCATION

For these reasons, undergraduate education in psychology is considered nonprofessional in nature. The position of the American Psychological Association, as expressed by various committees, conferences, and its Education and Training Board is that the undergraduate study of psychology has general educational value that gives it an important place in college curricula but that it cannot and should not attempt to prepare people for work as psychologists, except in laying a foundation for a higher degree.

Some colleges and universities do offer undergraduate courses that are professional in nature, but this practice is frowned upon. Instead it is recommended that undergraduate courses in psychology provide some of the theoretical understanding that is essential to the wise and effective use of professional techniques and that tool courses, such as those in intelligence testing, be offered only to persons who have the background necessary for the wise use of these tools. Furthermore, the need is stressed for the potential psychologist to include basic courses in other fields while an undergraduate, so that he or she will have the broad understanding needed as a foundation for professional education and for effective scientific and professional work.

Undergraduate study leading to career preparation as a psychologist should include a substantial amount of work in psychology (not necessarily a major). Such a program of study should be designed to give the student a fair acquaintance with the content of the field, both in its general and in its laboratory aspects. Courses in general, experimental, physiological, developmental, personality, social, educational, and metric psychology are desirable together with some work in the history of psychology. The emphasis and selection of these courses should vary with the theoretical or applied interests of the student, but there should be no heavy concentration at this stage.

The undergraduate who plans to become a psychologist should include in the program a substantial amount of work in the natural sciences, particularly in biology (including genetics). Some work in chemistry and physics also should be included, but the amount should vary with the ultimate objectives of the student and with the amount of physical science studied in high school. College work in mathematics and statistics, emphasizing principles, also should be included.

The social sciences should occupy an important part of the student's undergraduate program. Some students will emphasize natural science and others social science if they have clear ideas as to the field of psychology in which they will later specialize. For example, the future clinical psychologist may emphasize the biological sciences, the future counseling psychologist may stress the social sciences, and the future experimental psychologist may give equal emphasis to physiology and physics as a foundation for this specialty. All psychologists, however, should be well grounded in each of these fields. In the social sciences, sociology and anthropology seem most important, but economics, political science, and history also are relevant.

Literature, art, philosophy, and religion should not be neglected. Although these fields were somewhat looked down on by many psychologists a generation ago when psychology was striving to establish itself as a science, contemporary psychologists have become increasingly interested in what one can learn from these subjects about the needs and strivings of people. Humanistic psychology is one of the results of this interest. A good foundation in the humanities not only helps toward understanding human behavior but also enriches the life of the individual by adding to his or her personal resources.

Good writing and speaking skills are of vital importance. A psychologist, whether planning to be a teacher, research worker, clinician, or personnel administrator, must know how to organize and present facts and ideas in ways that are readily understood by and are interesting to a variety of audiences.

Finally, the student's undergraduate program should include experiences that help him or her to develop into an effective and interesting person. These experiences will vary widely because of differences in personality, interests, and abilities. They should include activities that enable the student to develop and use social skills in small groups, larger groups, and interpersonal relations. In addition, there should be activities that enlarge horizons and give familiarity with new fields of knowledge and new ways of life. Such an education will be useful whether or not the undergraduate eventually becomes a psychologist.

GRADUATE PREPARATION

Becoming a psychologist involves getting over a number of hurdles. The first of these is getting into college, and the second is graduating from college. Next comes getting into a graduate school, perhaps as a candidate for a master's degree, then obtaining the master's degree (a step skipped by many who aspire, on completing the B.A., to move directly to the doctorate). Then one must be accepted as a candidate for the doctorate, progress over several hurdles while in the doctoral program, and then pass a comprehensive examination, complete a doctoral dissertation or research project, and finally, in most universities, defend the doctoral dissertation in an oral examination. The number of people overcoming each hurdle gets smaller as the hurdles get higher. Several of these hurdles are more difficult to surmount than others, specifically, acceptance to a Ph.D., Psy.D., or Ed.D. program; passing the comprehensive examination for the doctorate; and completion of the doctoral dissertation. It is at these points that most of the candidates who do not succeed are dropped from the training programs.

Universities generally try to weed out the intellectually and emotionally unqualified as early as possible. They attempt to select only those students who are considered, at the time, likely to complete their studies. Moreover, the better universities seek to admit only as many students as can be handled effectively and, on completion of their studies, can be placed in appropriate jobs. Within these objectives, however, methods vary considerably, and it is well for the prospective student to know how the institution he or she is considering operates.

Selection of students for admission to master's and doctoral programs is based partly on intellectual ability as shown by college grades, achievement examinations, and scholastic aptitude tests. The Graduate Record Examination (achievement and aptitude) and the Miller Analogies Test (aptitude) were devised especially for these purposes. Ratings by college teachers also are used in an attempt to assess intellectual characteristics such as originality, resourcefulness, judgment, industriousness, motivation, and scholarliness.

Candidates for training in most of the applied or professional fields also are evaluated on their interest in people as individuals rather than as subjects for study. In addition, candidates are evaluated on their sensitivity to social situations, warmth, tact, insight, emotional stability, ethical standards, and other characteristics deemed especially important in fields in which the psychologist has considerable responsibility for and impact on people.

Candidates who are considering the teaching of psychology are likely to be judged by their obvious desire to share their knowledge with others, their skill in doing so, and their interest in keeping up with new developments.

Psychology students who are preparing for primarily scientific positions are generally judged by their interest in theory, that is, in the how and why of things. They also are judged on their concern for facts and on their skill and creativity in defining problems, in designing research, and in applying scientific methods to solutions.

Evidence of these characteristics generally is gathered during the course of graduate study as well as during undergraduate work. The first year often is designed partly to provide appropriate opportunities for judging. Undergraduate teachers also often know students well enough to make judgments concerning promise and performance in these areas and are skillful in setting up situations in which students can demonstrate these characteristics.

MASTER'S PROGRAMS

The degree Master of Arts (or Science or Education) requires one or two years of graduate study, varying with the institution or department. Most institutions believe that only average or better-than-average college students should be admitted to work for the M.A. Some institutions, however, admit any college graduate, and a few admit only potential doctoral candidates.

In the first two types of graduate schools, the master's program may be perceived as a proving ground for doctoral candidates in which students have a chance to show what they can do. It may be planned as a terminal program, designed to prepare students for work in some specialty. Or it may attempt to do both things at once. Many institutions that offer the master's degree do not offer programs for the doctorate. In this case, the student who wants to continue must apply to another institution and transfer on completion of the degree.

With such variations in M.A. programs, the student of psychology should know the program and policy of the institution being considered. First, does admission mean that one has been carefully screened and is considered a good doctoral risk? Does it mean that one's record has been evaluated and that one is considered a good risk for the M.A., with the idea that time will tell about the doctorate? Or does it merely mean that one is being allowed to find out whether or not one is really master's caliber?

Additionally, is one embarking on a program that will prepare the student for employment on completion of the M.A., or does the program have professional value only if the doctorate is completed? If the former is true, is the specialty one in which the student will be satisfied and in which employment prospects for M.A.s are good? As we have seen in Chapter 2, there are differences between fields: a master's degree in counseling, school psychology or measurement, for example, is more marketable than one in experimental or social psychology. If the latter is the case (and this is true of some excellent programs), what percentage of students completing the M.A. are able to continue toward the doctorate? Which type of program will be best for this student?

DOCTORAL PROGRAMS

The degree Doctor of Philosophy (or Psychology or Education) generally requires three or four years of graduate study, including the M.A., and often takes five years because of the time required for completing a research project. As already pointed out, completion of the M.A. is by no means a guarantee of admission to a doctorate program. In fact, admission to a doctorate program probably is the most difficult hurdle of all to surmount, and more would-be students are eliminated at that point than at any other. In fields such as clinical and counseling psychology, the ratio of applicants to openings ranges from 10 to 1 to as many as 40 to 1.

While some institutions consider it wise to use the master's program as a proving ground for doctoral work, most of the better universities consider it unwise to admit large numbers of candidates and weed out some during the first year of graduate study. Instead they prefer to admit as doctoral candidates only those whom they think are likely to complete their program of studies and to have them begin their graduate work as doctoral students. Transferring from an M.A. program to a Ph.D. program is difficult, if not impossible, in such institutions. Even then, the comprehensive examination still screens out some, and a few others fail to complete a dissertation. However, the student who is unsure of doctoral aspirations and abilities and who applies to a doctorate-granting institution for admission as a master's candidate (assuming it gives the M.A.) has the advantage of making his or her abilities known to the institution early in the course of graduate work. This makes possible more confident decisions concerning doctoral candidacy and may be better than applying with an M.A. from another institution. But the student who wants a doctorate and who is admitted directly to the program of a selective institution has a greater advantage: That student should be able to earn the degree and move directly toward that goal.

Doctoral programs, like master's programs, vary somewhat from one university to another. Some departments of psychology, for example, have long emphasized experimental psychology. In the past, some staff have contended that this should be the training of all psychologists, no matter what the later field of application is to be. On the other hand, other universities have for an equally long time emphasized the preparation of students equipped for intensive work in some of the special fields of psychology and thus have APA-approved programs in most of the applied fields.

These variations really are not as great as such a statement may make them seem. It is generally recognized that a psychologist should, first of all, be a psychologist and that specialization should represent expertness in—rather than limitation to—a special field. Thus the type of doctoral program approved by the Education and Training Board of the American Psychological Association today is one in which all doctoral candidates in psychology are well grounded in the basic courses and in which specialists in such fields as clinical, counseling, and school psychology are offered appropriate opportunities for the more advanced and intensive study of their specialties. These various fields of psychology, with the special training required, were described in Chapter 2.

POSTDOCTORAL PROGRAMS

Postdoctoral preparation in psychology has existed for many years in informal and unsystematic ways, but now it is formalized and more common in some specialties. College psychology teachers who wanted to shift to research or applied positions occasionally sought and obtained such positions at nominal salaries and with supervision, thus mastering the special skills and acquiring the special knowledge of the field to which they were changing. Today, postdoctoral training in clinical psychology is provided at centers such as the Postgraduate Center for Mental Health in New York and the Menninger Foundation in Topeka, in shorter courses given at some universities, and in connection with the annual meeting of the American Psychological Association.

Postdoctoral training in research is offered by a number of research institutes, many of them located at universities. The Social Science Research Council and the National Research Council have offered fellowships for a number of years for postdoctoral research training. The Ford Foundation, the National Science Foundation, and the Office of Education have contributed more recently to developments of this type. Similar developments are taking place in other special fields, but not as yet to the same extent as in clinical and experimental psychology, educational measurement, and research.

At all levels, students in the applied fields need opportunities to apply their knowledge and use their skills under expert supervision. This supervised experience is known as *practicum* training and generally is required in clinical, counseling, school, personnel, and applied social psychology. In many of the theoretical fields, such experience also is considered necessary, as in the laboratory work of the experimental psychologist, the nursery school and elementary school observation of the developmental psychologist, the field studies of the social psychologist, and the apprentice teaching of the graduate student with a teaching assistantship. While the American Psychological Association has not, through its Education and Training Board, recommended the inclusion of practicum training in many fields, the trend is very definitely in the direction of providing such training.

A student deciding on a university for graduate education should find out what types of practicum training (including research) are available. In the field of clinical psychology, for example, practicum training normally is preceded by laboratory training at the university in the use of psychological tests, interviewing, and observational techniques. It includes clerkship-level training in the application of these techniques to patients or clients who are being studied by fully qualified psychologists.

The second level of practicum training is internship experience in which the student studies and works with patients in a way which, by the end of the internship, approximates that of a junior staff member. In all of these activities, the work should be supervised; that is, the early testing should be observed and the test protocols corrected; later diagnostic reports should be reviewed and edited; psychotherapeutic work should be discussed (this last takes one-half hour or more of supervisory time for each hour spent with a patient); and relationships with clients and professional colleagues should be observed and reviewed.

CONTINUING EDUCATION

Psychologists, like professionals in many other areas, increasingly are interested in brief, intensive courses or workshops that are classified as "continuing education." Such programs may consist of a weekend seminar on new statistical techniques or an afternoon session on the psychologist's role in legal issues of criminal insanity. Many psychologists find continuing education workshops an efficient way to keep up with recent developments and acquire new skills. In addition, a certain number of hours at certified sessions is required by many states for keeping a valid license to practice psychology.

INSTITUTIONS OFFERING GRADUATE STUDY IN PSYCHOLOGY

One way to find out which institutions offer good programs of education for a science or profession is to get a list of those that have been accredited by the appropriate scientific or professional association. The scientific and professional association of psychology is the American Psychological Association. It has an Education and Training Board that coordinates the work of a number of committees dealing with special aspects of psychological training. One of these committees, created in 1947, formulated standards for the education of clinical psychologists because of requests from the United States Public Health Service and from the Veterans Administration. This committee then evaluated interested universities and prepared an approved list that these agencies could use in granting funds and in setting up training programs.

It has been the policy of the APA to evaluate and certify university departments of psychology only at the request of some outside organizations and cooperating universities. For this reason, there currently is no list of universities approved for the study of psychology in general. Instead there are lists of universities with approved doctoral programs only in clinical psychology, counseling psychology, and more recently, school psychology. While it is true that a department cannot be approved for training in these fields unless there is adequate supporting work in the basic fields, it is quite possible for a university to have excellent work in the basic fields and in some applied fields without offering a doctoral specialty in others.

Another way to evaluate universities would be by the number of degrees granted in the field of interest. Presumably a university that granted many degrees in psychology would necessarily be a university from which many people wanted degrees in psychology. But what people want depends partly on what they can get. Therefore, some universities award many degrees because their degrees are sought, while others awarding similar numbers may do so because they have low standards and admit many less able students. Similarly an institution granting few degrees may do so because of high standards, which lead it to accept only a few students to whom it offers superior resources, or it may grant few degrees because few people want a degree from that institution.

Furthermore, even within institutions there are differences, as shown by the fact that several universities have more than one department of psychology. In some of these universities, more than one department and in others only one department, are on approved lists. The larger number of degrees granted by a given university may then actually indicate that it has some good offerings and some poor offerings.

CHOOSING A GRADUATE SCHOOL

How then is the student to choose a university for graduate work in psychology? First, the student can use the APA-approved lists as guides for work in clinical, counseling, and school psychology and as indications that the institutions approved for work in these fields also have adequate supporting work in the basic fields. One should remember that some of the best work in fields other than the three evaluated fields is offered by universities that do not have applied psychology programs.

Second, one can judge also by the general reputation of the university in question as a graduate school, ascertaining its reputation among college faculty members of one's acquaintance and among psychologists with whom he or she has contact.

Third, one can use the Directory of the American Psychological Association or the American Psychological Society. They provide geographical directories that group psychologists by institutions; with the aid of these lists, one can look up individual psychologists in the alphabetical part of the directory in order to ascertain their training and experience levels. *American Men and Women of Science* can be used to check the published work of those prominent enough to be included in that directory.

Fourth, one can consult entries in the APA's *Graduate Study in Psychology,* published annually, to ascertain fields of specialization, financial aid, and other information about each university.

Fifth, one can browse through the *American Psychologist* and the *APA Monitor,* particularly the news items, in order to find out what is happening at various universities, who is conducting research projects, and where research grants are being funded. Presumably, foundations and the government give money and contracts to universities they have evaluated and found good for *their* purposes.

Sixth, one can look at the *Psychological Bulletin,* the *Annual Review of Psychology, Contemporary Psychology, Psychology Today,* and other psychological magazines and journals, reading reviews of research, book reviews, and other articles to see what kind of work is being done by university staff members and what other psychologists think of it.

The approved lists of the APA are published each year in the *American Psychologist;* these data usually are included in the November issue. The *Graduate Study in Psychology* publishes related data, such as the numbers of each kind of degree granted, the fields in which work is offered, admission procedures, and fellowships and stipends.

FINANCING GRADUATE EDUCATION

Finding the funds to finance from one to five years of graduate education often seems like a formidable task. With tuition ranging up to $15,000 per year or more, and the cost of room, meals, laundry, clothing, transportation, books, and supplies added to that, even the cost for one year easily amounts to $20,000 or more. One way of cutting down costs is, of course, to obtain a full-time job at or near the university and to go to classes on a part-time basis. This method, however, has the disadvantages of extending the amount of time you must spend on your education and preventing you from concentrating as only a full-time student can. Fellowships, loans, and assistantships generally are the answer. Institutions offering graduate work usually have a number of scholarships, fellowships, teaching assistantships, and research assistantships open to graduate students, as well as loan funds available without collateral. Some departments admit only students whom they can, in effect, support.

Scholarships and fellowships must be applied for in advance, usually in December, January, or February. They are awarded on a competitive basis, merit being judged by grades, examinations, and recommendations. They range from small scholarships granting exemption from tuition to more generous fellowships that provide full—if modest—support. These last fellowships are, of course, relatively scarce and much sought after. Information concerning such awards is given in university catalogs and is announced along with assistantships each year in *Graduate Study in Psychology* published by the APA. The university to which one is applying may be a very helpful source of information.

The United States Public Health Service has provided fellowships in clinical, child, physiological, and social psychology with stipends that vary with the level of training, plus tuition and fees. The Veterans Administration appoints students of clinical and counseling psychology to training positions in which they give about half time to a VA internship and half time to graduate study at stipends that also depend on training and experience. This does not include tuition. The Rehabilitation Services Administration provides traineeships for master's as well as for doctoral candidates at similar levels, with extras for tuition, fees, and dependents. These appointments are made by the university departments after the student has been admitted as a doctoral candidate. The National Science Foundation fellowships (for the basic fields in psychology) also provide good stipends, plus tuition, fees, and dependents' allowances. Application for these fellowships is made directly to the NSF.

Teaching assistantships usually are open only to students already in residence at a university and often are for small sums only. They may involve grading papers for a course with a stipend of a few hundred dollars for the semester. On the other hand, they may involve teaching sections of a large course at a stipend of several thousand dollars, sometimes with tuition exemption. In the long run, the experience often is as important as the stipend. It brings the student into more intimate contact with faculty members and introduces the student to the teaching profession.

Research assistantships sometimes are open to new students, but more often they are available only to those already in residence at a university. The duties involve working with faculty members and other research staff on research projects. These projects may be financed by grants from foundations, by institutional funds, or by industrial or government contracts. Half-time stipends range from $2,500 to $5,000 or more, often with free tuition. This type of financial assistance, like teaching assistantships, can have considerable educational value.

Loan funds exist at most universities and are often a crucial help during the first and last years of a student's work. During the first year, a student may need help while learning how to make ends meet; during the last year, financial help may enable the student to give the maximum possible amount of time to studies and research. Student loan funds usually have generous terms and are a good investment in a professional future.

Perhaps one of the most important facts to be remembered about financing advanced study is that an able student who has some resources for emergencies and something with which to start the academic year generally can find some way of financing graduate education, although changing government regulations for student loans have made this increasingly difficult. Nevertheless, over two-thirds of doctoral students in psychology received some kind of financial support for their studies.

A student will have to look well ahead of time into scholarships, fellowships, and teaching and research assistantships; the student may fall back, after registration, on part-time work; he or she may have to borrow; and many married students have been largely financed by a working spouse. It sometimes proves wise to work full-time for two or three years after the B.A. while saving funds for later full-time graduate study.

CHAPTER 6

A CAREER IN PSYCHOLOGY

A career, as defined by vocational psychologists (who may be counseling, clinical, or organizational in their professional affiliations), is not an occupation; it is a sequence of positions occupied by a person. *Occupations* are sets of tasks organized to constitute positions, with similar positions grouped to constitute an occupation. Occupations exist whether or not there are people to fill them, for they mean that a certain kind of work needs to be done to produce certain kinds of goods or services. *Careers* exist only in the lives of individuals. A career begins with education and the occupation of the position of student; it continues with work and the occupation of a sequence of positions that may or may not be substantively related. Thus a career in journalism may, and often used to, begin with employment as a copywriter and continue with promotion to reporter, then perhaps to editor or columnist. It now often begins with university study of English or journalism.

The current awareness of "mid-career crises," men's and women's occupational changes, and women's re-entry into the world of work after a period of full-time homemaking has made most people much more aware of career development problems and of the desirability of a longer-term perspective on career planning. This chapter, therefore, follows the chapter on education and training with discussions of getting started, getting ahead, and keeping up. It ends with a very brief consideration of eventual retirement, for in career development, it is usually "later than you think."

GETTING STARTED

Anyone aspiring to a profession should know what the profession is, what sort of work is done, where the work is done, what the future prospects are for the field, what kind of training will be needed to enter the profession, and where to get this training. In addition, he or she also must know how to get started and become established in the chosen profession. The majority of these topics—job analysis and description, social and economic trends, training—are relatively objective and hence easily dealt with. But getting started and getting established in a profession is another matter. It is a social and psychological process with many variations and is much more difficult to observe and to analyze.

Those who engage in an occupation are often somewhat reluctant to look at it objectively, because a careful analysis may make certain aspects appear in an unfavorable light. Furthermore, not all writers on occupations are trained and experienced in the methods of observing and analyzing human behavior. In recent years, psychologists and sociologists have been paying more attention to the process of entering and gaining a foothold in an occupation.

It is therefore possible at present to describe some of the principal methods for making a place for oneself in a profession such as psychology. The reader of this description should not, however, get the impression that psychologists are any more success-minded than other professional groups. Each occupation has its own version of the ways of getting ahead described here. The emphasis on success is as much a part of our civilization as is the emphasis on human welfare. Psychologists as a group tend to emphasize human values rather than material values. This is exemplified by their code of ethics, which stresses their obligations to society more than their obligations to each other. The code is not a means of defending the selfish interests of the profession, but rather it is one method of protecting the genuine interests of the public.

Personal Evaluation

The student of psychology who is about to complete formal professional education, whether at the M.A. or Ph.D. level, is a merchandiser about to put a new product on the market. The new psychologist has a product to sell: oneself, or rather, one's professional services. The new psychologist must analyze this product to see what there is about it people might want, find a market that wants this product, and find out how to get this product to that market in a way that makes people want it.

In analyzing the product, a budding psychologist should review educational, avocational, and vocational experiences to see what he or she can offer in the way of psychological services that other people want. What, as a teacher, researcher, clinician, counselor, or administrator does the prospective applicant have in the way of assets? Has the student been a graduate assistant with teaching responsibilities? If so, this is a vocational asset. Was the teaching assistantship in association with a psychologist who had something of a reputation as a teacher? If the answer is yes, perhaps the student caught some of the sponsor's inspiration, and this, too, is an asset to be used. Did the student participate in any research activities independently of the thesis? These should be considered as a sign of breadth of experience, originality, and research ability. Were these research activities carried on in collaboration with a famous research psychologist, and did they result in publication? More assets! Did the student have an internship in a clinic or research institute with a reputation for high standards and good work? Did he or she win the esteem of supervisors and colleagues during this internship? This also is something that may have market value. Did the student participate in any nonpsychological activities that might show creative ability, leadership, or culture? These things are valued in college teachers, research workers, clinicians, and administrators.

The purpose of listing assets is, of course, to examine them to see to whom they might be of value and how. They may point up college teaching (the successful teaching assistant), public school work (the former teacher), market research (the former business major), research on international communication (the social psychologist who spent time in the Far East), or counseling in a community agency (the homemaker who raised a family, was active in the PTA, and served on social agency boards). The wise student has, of course, planned his or her education and training with a special market in view so that when he or she prepares to seek a position, it is done with knowledge of self and knowledge of the market.

A survey of the job market can be accomplished easily after a student has analyzed his or her training and experience. A job aspirant can locate potential positions by reviewing items in professional journals such as the *American Psychologist* and the *APA Monitor,* by noting items concerning employing agencies in the general news, and by talking with faculty members, practicum supervisors, and friends about developments that may have significance for employment.

Good examples of such developments are the prestige of the military psychology programs in World War II, combined with the obvious contributions of research in the physical sciences, which made it almost inevitable that psychologists who combined research and administrative ability with military experience would find a ready market for their services in government research after the war. The Korean and Vietnam Wars meant a strengthening of the Veterans Administration vocational counseling program in regional offices and contract centers. The strengthening of higher education in the South has provided more positions for well-trained college teachers whose southern connections make it likely that they will be glad to find a worthwhile career there rather than stay (as all too frequently happens) in the northern institutions in which psychologists have tended to do their graduate work. The proliferation of community colleges means that more teachers, counselors, and deans will be required. The development of the antipoverty programs added greatly to the demand for educational, social, counseling, and measurement psychologists. The rapid growth of human services has prepared openings for large numbers of psychologists providing health services.

An informal survey of developments in psychology, education, welfare work, medicine, industry, government, and the armed forces yields suggestions as to where the young psychologist finishing graduate studies may best market his or her services.

Making oneself available is done in a variety of ways, some subtle, some obvious, all appropriate in their proper places. The less obvious ways consist of publishing minor research and reading papers at psychological meetings while still a student; taking on short-term and vacation jobs that bring one in contact with potential employers and with people who know employers; attending professional meetings and taking advantage of (without abusing) the occasional opportunities that arise to increase one's acquaintance among psychologists; and getting to know the members of one's own department as well as possible so that one is thought of when openings are available.

One psychologist employed in a large-scale research program was offered his position because of a paper he read at a national convention while a graduate student. This paper caught the attention of the psychologist who later headed up the research program. Another obtained her position as a college professor because, at another convention, she joined a friend at breakfast. This friend happened to be sitting with a third psychologist who was looking for a new assistant professor. Still another psychologist is director of a college counseling center because he accepted a minor assistantship while a graduate student. He carried out his routine duties in a way that made him stand out in the minds of the faculty as a person of unusual ability. Finally, a young woman in the male-dominated field of industrial psychology got her start in industry by working on a professor's research, which took them into several business organizations.

Placement Services

Registering with a placement service is another, more obvious, and very acceptable method of making oneself available to employers. Most universities operate placement offices in which student and alumni records are kept and to which employers write about openings. Many faculty members operate informal placement services, keeping lists or sets of resumes of students and former students interested in jobs. Some professors, research workers, and practitioners with reputations receive many requests for nominations to jobs from employers who know them or their work. Having papers on file in the placement office makes it easy for a professor to recommend someone with supporting evidence.

The American Psychological Association operates a placement service, listing positions available and positions wanted in a monthly employment section of the *APA Monitor,* which is sent to all members and to many libraries. The *Observer* of the American Psychological Society also lists employment openings. Large professional meetings, such as the annual national convention of the American Psychological Association, also provide placement services and facilitate interviews. The state employment offices in some states operate placement services for psychologists in their professional divisions. Finally, federal and state civil service examinations offer another means for the psychologists in search of employment. There often are openings in the federal civil service for research psychologists with physiological, experimental, social, psychometric, personnel, clinical, and counseling specialties.

Resumes and Applications

A final technique for finding employment is the preparation of a resume. The resume should include the psychologist's education and experience and be designed so as to point up suitability for a certain type of employment. This resume may be mailed with a cover letter to selected potential employers, but such mailing must be handled very selectively and sometimes is better done by a professor in the student's major area than by the student. More importantly, however, the major route of job application in the past decade or two has become formal response to public notice of openings in, for example, the placement services noted above and through college and university placement offices. This trend toward announcement and response, rather than solicitation and invitation, is primarily the result of equal opportunity legislation and changing ethics. However, the supply and demand ratio, tipping more heavily toward supply, has had an effect as well. In any case, the resume is an important introduction to the potential employer, to be used in making applications and seeking positions. A number of books on job-seeking deal with the techniques of preparing resumes so that the product is effectively introduced to the prospective buyer.

Personal Interviews

Techniques of applying for positions in person also are dealt with in such manuals, but there are certain customs in the employment of psychologists that the student should be aware of. Colleges and universities like to observe certain traditions of gentility, even though they may actually engage in hard-headed bargaining. For example, the major universities have a way of not putting themselves in the position of being turned down by candidates for employment. They sometimes achieve this by asking the candidates, late in the explorations, whether, if offered the position at such and such a salary, they would accept.

The colleges expect the applicants, too, to be above bargaining. The applicants achieve this by knowing ahead of time what salary they can command and what salary the college is likely to be able to pay. Candidates also let the college know in various subtle ways that they know what they are worth. The university is likely to offer a position to a candidate in the first place only if it has been led by its own analysis to believe that what it is interested in paying is what the candidate believes he or she is worth or feels forced by circumstances to accept.

The hiring processes in medical, social work, governmental, and industrial settings are different in some respects from those in colleges and universities. They are generally more formalized; salaries in governmental organizations are more pre-set, in business more negotiable.

A Good Start

Getting off to a good start in the new position, like applying for the position, requires a knowledge of and respect for ways of doing things. The psychologist working in governmental or industrial bureaucracy must know the official channels through which business is transacted. The researcher who works in a large insurance company must know in which of the company dining rooms to eat and not be overly bothered by social stratification. The college instructor must be able to see a challenge rather than an insult in the immaturity of some of the students. And each type of situation has its "uniform," be it a sober business suit or blue jeans.

The undergraduate student may have limited horizons and lack intellectual curiosity. The business executive may be interested in answers that give results rather than in methods that give answers. The military officer may desire results immediately if not sooner. The patient may refuse to conform to textbook types. The medical specialist may have more confidence in the conclusions that he or she reached after working with one case than in those that someone else drew from a statistical analysis of one hundred cases. These are just a few of the more serious and more constant challenges that the newly employed psychologist must accept graciously and learn to handle to keep the job and render the type of service that will make the job worth keeping.

GETTING AHEAD

Once the psychologist is at work on the new job and has made the initial adjustments to become part of the institution in which he or she works, the next problem to be faced is that of getting ahead. It probably is desirable to remain in a position for at least two or three years to demonstrate that one is stable and dependable as well as to provide some real service to the employer to justify the expense of "breaking in." At the same time, the employee should plan some activities that will pave the way for promotion or for offers of better positions. If one plans wisely, doing justice to the job, to the profession, and to the public, one also will add to one's professional stature. For example, like other scientists and professional people, the psychologist has a responsibility for keeping up with new developments in the field. The rapid progress being made by psychology makes this a real chore; the volume of newly published research is great. It is the responsibility of the psychologist to read, interpret, and apply this new knowledge at work.

The means most typically used by psychologists to bring about advancement are teaching, writing, research, practice (application), professional activity (committee work and office holding), and popularization. These are not all equally effective nor equally esteemed, but all are used.

Teaching

In a field that includes both pure and applied science, university connections and university teaching confer prestige. Universities tend to seek faculty members who have excelled in some aspect of their scientific or professional work. These are presumably the women and men who have something to contribute to students, who will attract new students, and who will in other ways help build up the institution. Reasoning conversely, having a teaching appointment in a university is often assumed, rightly or wrongly, to be a sign of attainment.

The prestige of university connections makes part-time teaching appointments a means by which psychologists working in clinics, hospitals, counseling centers, schools, industry, and government agencies advance in their fields. Those who can teach others well to do what they have done well add to their professional stature and make themselves known to a larger audience of psychologists and other consumers of psychological knowledge. They make their wisdom and skill known to others in a highly acceptable way. They also tend to enjoy sharing their knowledge with interested students.

Psychologists who are full-time instructors or professors are in a position to build reputations as teachers. They are able to organize and conduct courses in such a way as to attract students who will want to study with them because their instruction is meaningful and helpful. In some institutions it may be that attracting large numbers is important, for numbers mean fees and financial support to poorly endowed institutions. In others it is not so much quantity as quality that counts, and the teacher who attracts outstanding students, students who make their mark on the field, is the teacher who comes, in due course, to be valued. Such instructors get recognition and advancement when other universities and institutions bid for their services and when their own institutions try to keep them.

Good teaching does not just happen, and good teachers are not all good in the same way. The ability to synthesize and interpret the knowledge of one's field, both theory and research, is an important component. Well-motivated students will learn from a good synthesizer, even though he or she may be a boring lecturer. The ability to present knowledge, whether in lectures, projects, or other less traditional ways also is an important quality in teaching. Although the substance of a field may be well learned in graduate school, the ability to teach too often is not developed in doctoral programs, nor is it acquired automatically by observation. This is especially true if role models are not the best and if, no matter what their quality, available role models are not studied with improvement or emulation in mind. Graduate students are graded on their command of the substance and methodology of their field, not on their ability to teach them; they therefore concentrate on substance and on scientific or professional methods.

A wise student pays some attention to how professors teach, finds opportunities to assist in teaching, and seeks suggestions and criticism of his or her performance with an eye to improvement. Psychologists who win distinction as teachers do so only with some effort and after a period of unofficial internship in teaching, including their first years as teachers. Obtaining class evaluations, very common since the late 1960s, provides helpful material, especially if one recognizes that good teaching for one student may not be good teaching for another. The evaluation of fellow instructors also can be helpful.

The ability to synthesize and present in the classroom or laboratory can contribute to one's reputation not only on the campus but beyond it; some of the best and most widely used textbooks have been produced by instructors who developed their own materials, tried them out on their own students, improved them with field trial, and then published them with resulting national recognition.

However, superior teaching, important as it is to colleges and universities, often is not enough to bring advancement. A teacher's reputation generally does not spread rapidly, and when it does spread it is in quiet ways that may not come immediately to the attention of administrators. Unless offers from other institutions are forthcoming, good teaching brings promotion slowly.

Publication

Publication, on the other hand, whether in the form of textbooks, research monographs, articles in professional and scientific journals, or papers at scientific meetings, attracts attention more rapidly. It is tangible, and its results can be brought together and examined for quantity and quality. A study that is frequently quoted in textbooks, a text that is used in many institutions, or even a number of journal articles that may have limited intrinsic value, have the effect of publicizing both the institution at which the psychologist works and the psychologist personally. The psychologist thus becomes well known, and if the publications have been genuine contributions rather than chaff, this reputation brings students, clients, grants, contracts, offers of positions, and promotions. For academic psychologists, those in research positions, and those employed in medical, community, governmental, or industrial settings, this is a superior and satisfying way in which to develop a reputation among other psychologists and among kindred professionals and executives.

Research

Research is closely related to publication as a means of advancement. Research usually will result in publication, but it is different in some respects. Developing a reputation as a writer may be achieved through textbooks, reviews, or other contributions not based on original research or experimentation. Research may lead only to rare monographs, articles, and papers, but it may be so important that its impact is great. The nature and scope of a project may capture the imagination of others. Its planning may be so well conceived and its initial stages so well carried out that the psychologists involved in the project will acquire reputations as research workers even before any significant publications result from their work.

The emphasis on scientific method and the interest in functioning as a scientific profession that characterize modern psychology tend to make research and writing the methods *par excellence* for establishing a reputation and for advancing in the field. They are methods that are very satisfying to an intellectually curious, research-minded person.

Development Work

The practice of psychology is another means of advancement that is becoming increasingly important as the demand for psychological services increases and as the number of psychological practitioners becomes greater. Engineering, measurement, school, counseling, personnel, or applied social psychologists who are especially effective in development work in business, the armed forces, or education find their services very much in demand.

The term *development* may need a little explanation. It frequently is used in connection with the term *research*. The development of a proficiency examination for policemen or for computer programmers, for example, is not research in the strict sense of the word. It involves no new contributions to knowledge but is simply the application of existing techniques to a slightly different problem. It is, however, a task best carried out or supervised by persons with a research background and research skills.

Similarly, making a follow-up study of students who have left high school in order to get data for use in revising the offerings of the school involves no new techniques and contributes no new fundamental knowledge. It is, again, the kind of project to which a research-trained educational, counseling, or personnel psychologist can contribute a great deal in rationale, method, and interpretation.

A number of consulting organizations and research institutes specialize in this type of work, and many college teachers are active consultants on such projects. Those who are skillful in working with others to put existing knowledge to work find themselves valued as staff members and as consultants, and thus they become established rapidly.

Clinical and Counseling Work

The practice of psychology, however, is not limited to development work. In fact, it is the clinical and counseling applications of psychology that traditionally have been best known. They, too, have been very much in demand; as a result, competent clinicians and counselors have found ample opportunity to advance to responsible positions or to develop private practices.

The practicing clinical or counseling psychologist, like other psychologists, may build a reputation partly through publication, research, and teaching, but in practice these are incidental or peripheral activities. Their principal functions are diagnosis, assessment, psychotherapy, and counseling. The practitioner therefore develops a reputation among professional colleagues and among clients by establishing and maintaining good interpersonal relations, by becoming a skillful diagnostician, by doing an effective job of counseling or psychotherapy, and by communicating with colleagues in psychology and in the related professions in ways that are meaningful to them. The practitioners' services are valued because social workers find that their case summaries provide a sound and clear basis for child placement, because pediatricians find them good team members in working with difficult children and parents, because psychiatrists find their diagnostic summaries perceptive and to the point, and because teachers feel that they understand school problems and help show how classroom situations can be used to help children. It is those who are effective in this type of work who are offered opportunities for supervisory and administrative responsibility.

Committee Work

Committee work often proves to be an important means of bringing to light a psychologist's ability and contributions. This is especially true in the case of teachers whose superior teaching builds reputations rather slowly, and in the case of clinicians and counselors whose effective work with clients and professional colleagues may remain known only in the relatively limited circles of their institutions. The American Psychological Association, the American Psychological Society, the various state psychological associations, and some city associations have a large number of active committees working on a variety of scientific and professional problems. The burden of committee work falls heavily on those who have the ability and the motivation to work, so that new talent is eagerly sought and soon given responsibility.

Popularization

Popularization (writing or talking about psychology for the general public) is another method that sometimes is used by psychologists to build reputations and to advance. Traditionally, however, this has not been viewed very favorably by the profession unless it is incidental to substantive contributions or done by professional writers. The fact that psychology has a strong popular appeal makes for quite a demand for popularization in widely read magazines, popular books, newspaper stories, radio, television, and public lectures. The very nature of the appeal, however, often results in the distortion of psychological data, selection of the sensational, and catering to unhealthy needs and interests.

Popularization of a type that is in the public interest requires a great deal of skill, time, and strength of mind on the part of the psychologist. Many popularizers have found their best efforts frustrated by a sales-minded publisher or TV producer. An occasional psychologist has violated the APA's Code of Ethics and fallen from grace because the lure of easy money through popular writing and lecturing led the psychologist to cater to publicity and sales departments. Another important factor is the tendency of scientists to be skeptical of popularizers, even though it is in the interest of a science or a profession to have its work understood and supported by the public. The American Psychological Association and the American Psychological Society are very much aware of the need for good popularization, and publishers, press, radio, and television are receptive to good popularization. There is growing interest in psychology for these media, but abuses still make it a rather difficult way for a young psychologist to make a solid reputation or to win advancement.

MOVING AHEAD

The American dream has always been to find something better. Moving from one place to another, from one job to another, even from one occupation to another often has been viewed as the means. Even if one really likes the present job, the present institution or organization, and the present place of residence, distant pastures may seem greener.

Americans were a very mobile people during the decades immediately following each major war, and the tradition of mobility persists even during periods of recession and depression. One good reason for doing graduate work in a university other than that in which the bachelor's degree was earned is that one can thus get a broader perspective on higher education as a place of employment. Similarly one good reason for field work and internship is to learn in greater depth what psychologists do in a variety of settings.

Mobility is not necessarily a good thing, but having other employers want to hire one often does help to make a person seem valued at one's own institution or organization. The potential of mobility is good, provided it does not make one restless and distracted from the work at hand. The means of making oneself wanted already have been discussed. In this section, attention is paid to the types of mobility that are typical of psychologists.

Academic Networks

Each graduate school tends to have its network of communicating, mutually respecting, and accepting institutions. The foundations of these networks are partly geographic, for people from neighboring institutions meet more readily, for example, at the annual Eastern, Southeastern, Midwestern and Western Psychological Association meetings. They are partly affiliational, for people tend to maintain contact with their former professors, their fellow graduate students, and their own former students. And they are partly hierarchical—prestige-based—for the famous universities tend to place their graduates in other well-known institutions, and the universities with local reputations, no matter how good, tend to place their graduates in nearby, often lesser, institutions.

There are thus several academic networks, and movement tends to be within the network in which one starts academic work. People do move from higher-level networks to lower, sometimes because of the attractions of less famous but in other ways very attractive colleges or universities, or sometimes because of the lack of openings in the favored network. Movement from a lower-level network to a higher one is less common and is most likely to be the result of unusually good research or writing. In the applied fields, and this is less often the case, it may be the result of unusual contributions in the development of service programs or in professional committee work. Some graduate schools make a practice of employing their best graduates in junior positions after they get their degrees—a help in getting teaching experience—while others prefer to see them go elsewhere and prove their worth in the field before considering them for teaching appointments. Those who stay at their alma mater too often have a rude awakening when they are pushed out of the nest after four or five years of service to make room for another, newer, candidate for whom tenure will not be a question for several years. The possibilities of getting tenure are important in considering a first regular academic appointment, and getting onto a tenure track at least one or two years after receiving a graduate degree generally is wise in academia.

Practitioner Networks

Careers in private practice may, of course, involve consultation either with individuals (clinical or counseling) or organizations (industrial and organizational, including assessment, counseling, and organizational and group development). Practitioners not only work alone, as has so commonly been true of physicians and dentists, but often in groups as has been true of lawyers and is increasingly true of physicians. It is clinicians and counselors who are most likely to eventually work on their own with private patients or clients, while some, like most industrial and organizational psychologists who engage in consulting work, do so within an organizational framework. The common pattern for those interested in being practitioners is to start in a junior staff position in such an institutional or organizational setting, partly to develop expertise and partly to accumulate evidence of legitimacy and competence. From a university, business, industrial, or consulting firm base, the neophyte develops not only competence and contacts but also the maturity essential for public confidence. If interested, they then can move to full-time practice on their own or in higher-level organizational work.

Reputations as practitioners develop largely through word of mouth, personal contacts, training workshops, and work well done. Getting ahead is measured first in the type of work that one is assigned, then in terms of the type of problems on which one is asked to consult and on the volume of work or business that one develops, whether within the framework of an organization or on one's own.

It may at first seem odd that clinical and industrial practice are dealt with together, as they are here. The reason lies not only in the fact that both are applied fields, but also because people in either clinical or industrial practice do need to start in an institutional setting, unless they can gamble for some time while building a practice. The networks are distinct, but their patterns are similar.

THINK TANKS, RESEARCH INSTITUTES, AND FREELANCE

A small but growing number of psychologists carry out research outside the academic setting in think tanks or research institutes such as the American Institutes for Research, or freelancing on their own. Such work is similar in many ways to academic research, often resulting in professional publication as well as a final report to the client (a government funding agency, private foundation that supports research, or perhaps a business firm). Usually the research is directed to specific problems in the nonacademic world. In many ways, however, psychologists in these networks forge careers that resemble those of practitioners; their work is oriented to a "product" rather than teaching and pure knowledge, and their networks of colleagues and potential employers again are distinct. This group of hybrid occupations has emerged for a variety of economic and structural reasons and is still in the process of defining its niche between the academic and the traditional practice.

The Linkage Systems

Linkages between the academic, practitioner, and research networks are limited once the graduate student has left the university, and they are infrequently used; it is essentially a one-way street. Academic psychologists who, because of their research, writing, or teaching, are perceived by business, industry, institutes, or government as having contributions to make to practice may develop part-time consulting work and perhaps be in a position to receive or seek offers of positions. An occasional practitioner (whether clinical, counseling, or industrial and organizational) or researcher may be offered an academic post so that students can have the benefit of one or more full-time professors with strong applied backgrounds. But such instances are exceptional.

The higher incomes of successful practitioners do sometimes tempt the academics. Conversely, the greater security of academe sometimes tempts the psychologist in business or industry. The greater freedom of university work may tempt the industrial, business, or government employee or other practitioner who feels tied down by office hours. Or the risks and challenges of applied work may tempt the teacher tired of grading papers or of degree seekers who are not interested in knowledge. Each person considering a career in psychology should take into account that this great variety of options is available and that what is a wise choice for one person may not be a wise choice for another. Exploration of the possibilities is called for while still in college and graduate school so that the graduate program can be planned with emphases that qualify one for the desired type of career in psychology.

THE LAST STAGE OF A CAREER: RETIREMENT

People rarely, if ever, choose a career because of its retirement possibilities, but it is good to have some notion of what they may be.

As members of a profession, psychologists have access to the same types of retirement benefits that other professionals have: Social Security, self-financed retirement annuity plans, the Carnegie-founded Teachers Insurance Annuity Association and related funds if employed by a university, and other organizational retirement plans if employed by business, industry, or government.

Psychologists also share with other scientists and professionals interests that not only find expression in their work but also frequently and readily find outlets in their hobbies and leisure-time activities. These can carry over into retirement whether as work or play. This is of considerable psychological importance and has been related to longevity. The pursuit of such activities often develops enduring friendships. Thus part-time work, hobbies, and friendships give life after retirement continued meaning and provide the *raison d'etre* that leads to a long and enjoyable life after retirement.

CHAPTER 7

SCIENTIFIC AND PROFESSIONAL ORGANIZATIONS IN PSYCHOLOGY

For more than one hundred years, the primary professional and scientific association for psychologists in North America has been the American Psychological Association (APA). (There is also a much younger, Canadian Psychological Association, but many Canadian psychologists also belong to the American association.) There are a number of smaller, more narrowly focused associations, such as the Psychonomic Society, and many psychologists also belong to related professional societies such as the American Educational Research Association—some of these are listed later in this chapter.

The American Psychological Society (APS) was formed largely by members of the APA who were unhappy with what they perceived as a slighting of scientific concerns in favor of professional or health provider ones. The APS has grown rapidly and developed a number of new activities. At the same time, the APA has responded innovatively to many of the criticisms from academic psychologists and has maintained its high level of professional representation in the public domain, especially with regard to health care policy reform. Many psychologists are members of both organizations.

THE AMERICAN PSYCHOLOGICAL ASSOCIATION

The American Psychological Association has its headquarters in its own building at 750 First Street NE, Washington, DC 20002-4242. The APA also has an extensive website at www.apa.org. There you'll find information on the APA and its divisions and also the following information:

accredited schools/programs
boards and committees
books
careers
conferences
continuing education
conventions
international affairs
jobs
journals
licensure
pamphlets
position papers
publications and communications
research funding
research office
salary surveys
state associations

But that doesn't even scratch the surface. A visit to the APA website is a must for any potential psychology major.

The APA has a staff consisting of a full-time executive secretary, a managing editor for its journals, and others concerned with professional education and placement. Its affairs are directed by an elected president, other officers, and a board of directors. In addition, there is a larger council of representatives elected by the various divisions of the association. Much of the association's work is carried out by boards and committees, some of which are listed here.

Selected Boards and Committees of the American Psychological Association

Board for the Advancement of Psychology in the Public Interest
Board of Convention Affairs
Board of Educational Affairs
Board of Professional Affairs
Board of Scientific Affairs
Election Committee
Ethics Committee

Finance Committee
Membership Committee
Committee on Accreditation
Committee on Aging
Committee on Animal Research and Ethics
Committee on Children, Youth, and Families
Committee on Disability Issues in Psychology
Committee on Division/APA Relations
Committee on Ethnic Minority Affairs
Committee on International Relations in Psychology
Committee on Lesbian, Gay, and Bisexual Concerns
Committee on Professional Practice and Standards
Committee on Psychological Tests and Assessment
Committee on Rural Health

The special interests of psychologists in the American Psychological Association are served by fifty-three divisions. Each division is concerned either with a special aspect of psychology as a science, with the applications of psychology in some special field, or with the interests of psychologists employed in a particular type of setting.

There are currently more than 159,000 members of the American Psychological Association, much greater than ten years ago. The increase has resulted largely from the rapid growth of psychologists providing health services. But the growth and particularly the shift toward psychology as a health profession created great tensions within the association about how best to organize its affairs for promoting both the science and the practice of psychology. As a result, a large number of psychologists formed the new American Psychological Society. Many of these were based in university or research institutions and were oriented to the science side of psychology, although many of them also had applied, if not clinical, interests. A large number maintain membership in both organizations.

Members of the American Psychological Association may be either associates, members, or fellows. Associates must have completed either two years of graduate study in psychology in a recognized graduate school or one year of graduate study plus one year of experience in work that is psychological in nature. In both cases, at the time of application they must be devoted full-time to professional or graduate work that is psychological in nature. Associates do not vote or hold office.

Members must have a doctorate in psychology based in part on a psychological dissertation or from a program primarily psychological in content and obtained at a recognized graduate school.

Fellows of the APA must have a doctoral degree based in part on a psychological dissertation conferred by a graduate school of recognized standing. They must have been members for at least a year, must have had five years of acceptable professional experience after receiving the doctorate, and must, after nomination by a division of the APA, present evidence of unusual and outstanding contribution or performance in psychology.

Dues to the association range from $54 to $215 a year. Students are eligible for special affiliation at greatly reduced rates. These dues include a subscription to the official journal of the APA, the *American Psychologist,* and the *APA Monitor* (monthly newspaper). In addition, other regular scientific and professional journals are published. Annual conventions are held in a different city each year in late August or early September.

In addition to the national association, there are regional, state, and local associations that meet regularly to hear scientific papers, to discuss problems of common interest, and occasionally to take action on professional matters. The regional and state associations usually limit their activities to one meeting each year.

The American Psychological Association also can provide information about related groups within psychology that focus on special concerns. Contact the appropriate office, c/o American Psychological Association, 750 First Street NE, Washington, DC 20002-4242 or visit www.apa.org.

THE AMERICAN PSYCHOLOGICAL SOCIETY

The American Psychological Society was founded in 1988 and now has more than fifteen thousand members. It currently publishes three journals, *Psychological Science,* which carries articles on research, theory, and applications in psychology and related behavioral, cognitive, neural, and social sciences; *Current Directions in Psychological Science,* which features summaries and reviews of recent trends and controversies in a manner that is accessible to a wider audience of readers both within and outside the discipline; and *Psychological Science in the Public Interest,* published twice a year as a supplement to *Psychological Science.* The APS also publishes a monthly newsletter, the *Observer.* There is an annual meeting of the society, at which numerous symposia and reports of scientific studies are presented. The society's headquarters and editorial offices are at 1010 Vermont Avenue NW, Suite 1100, Washington, DC 20005-4907. Their website is located at www.psychologicalscience.org.

THE AMERICAN BOARD OF EXAMINERS IN PROFESSIONAL PSYCHOLOGY

The American Board of Examiners in Professional Psychology is appointed from a list of leading psychologists nominated by the American Psychological Association. It is separately incorporated. The board is responsible for examining and certifying psychologists in the professional fields and issues diplomas in clinical, counseling, and industrial psychology.

Diplomates, as the holders of these diplomas are called, must have held a doctorate in psychology with appropriate specialization for at least five years. In addition, they must have experience in their specialty, meet high ethical standards, and pass written, oral, and practical examinations in the general field of psychology and in their specialty.

The work of this board, therefore, makes it easy for the public to identify practicing psychologists who are clearly recognized by their fellows as having attained a high level of competence and who have adhered to high levels of ethical standards. The publication of a directory of approved psychological service centers is the function of the American Board for Psychological Services. Several other boards exist for special purposes.

PSI CHI

Psi Chi is the national honor society in psychology with chapters on the campuses of many colleges and universities. It holds meetings like those of the state and local associations and helps with the orientation of psychology students to their field, but its main purpose is to encourage students to maintain excellence in psychology and advance the science of psychology. For information about activities and membership, write to Psi Chi, 825 Vine Street, Chattanooga, TN 37403-0709 or visit www.psichi.org/content.

RELATED ASSOCIATIONS

There are a number of other scientific and professional societies that include psychological divisions or in which psychologists and members of related fields meet. These include the following:

The American Association for the Advancement of Science
The American Association on Mental Deficiency
The American Educational Research Association
The American Management Association
The American Orthopsychiatric Association
The American Personnel and Guidance Association
The Association for the Advancement of Psychology
The Canadian Psychological Association
The International Association of Applied Psychology
The International Association for Cross-Cultural Psychology
The International Society of Political Psychology
The National Association of School Psychologists
The National Education Association
The Psychonomic Society

STATE LICENSING AND CERTIFICATION BOARDS

All states and Canadian provinces have laws for the licensing or certification of psychologists. A licensing law requires that anyone performing certain types of services be licensed by the state. A certification law prohibits anyone from using a specified occupational title unless he or she has been certified as qualified by the state.

The states of California, Georgia, Kentucky, Minnesota, Tennessee, and Virginia are among those that have licensing laws for psychologists or for certain specialists in psychology. Connecticut, Kansas, and New York are examples of states that have certification laws.

A board of psychologists appointed by the governor, on recommendation of the state department, handles certification and licensing and reviews and examines applicants. Psychologists expecting to work in a given state should ascertain the status of licensing in that state, the nature of the requirements where such exist, and the procedure for complying. Such information is usually available from state departments of education and also may be obtained from the secretaries of the state psychological associations. The American Psychological Association and its *Biographical Directory* are sources of such information. Also contact the Association of State and Provincial Psychology Boards, P.O. Box 4589, Montgomery, AL 36103-4589 or visit their website at www.asppb.org.

THE COUNCIL FOR THE NATIONAL REGISTER OF HEALTH SERVICE PROVIDERS IN PSYCHOLOGY

Since 1975 the council, an independent corporation, has published the *National Register of Health Service Providers in Psychology.* This is a voluntary listing of psychologists who meet specified criteria as health service providers, but it is emerging as a valuable central registry of human resources in the converging specialties that constitute "health psychology" (primarily clinical, counseling, and school psychology). The *Register* lists more than fifteen thousand psychologists who are certified or licensed for independent practice in their states and who are duly trained and experienced in the delivery of direct, preventive, assessment, and therapeutic intervention services to individuals whose growth, adjustment, or functioning is actually impaired or is demonstrably at high risk of impairment.

RECOMMENDED READING

The following books are published by the American Psychological Association. For complete book descriptions and ordering information visit the APA website at www.apa.org/books/students.html or call 1-800-374-2721.

Career Paths in Psychology: Where Your Degree Can Take You, by Robert J. Sternberg, 1997.

Critical Thinking About Research: Psychology and Related Fields, by Julian Meltzoff, 1998. Equips you with the tools needed to identify errors in others' research and to reduce them to a minimum in your own work.

Dissertations and Theses from Start to Finish: Psychology and Related Fields, by John D. Cone and Sharon L. Foster, 1993.

Encyclopedia of Psychology: 8 Volume Set, by Alan E. Kazdin, Ph.D., Editor-in-Chief, 2000. Definitive guide to every area of psychological theory, research, and practice.

Getting In: A Step-by-Step Plan for Gaining Admission to Graduate School in Psychology, 1993. Competition is fierce and admission standards are high. *Getting In* reduces the stress of applying and increases applicants' chances of being accepted in the programs of their choice. Applicants are provided with manageable goals and the tools to achieve them. Among the tools are a monthly timetable for completing application tasks, concrete information about career options in psychology, descriptions of graduate specialty options, and detailed worksheets for selecting the best program matches.

Graduate Study in Psychology: 2000 Edition. Print and electronic versions. Offers practical information about more than five hundred psychology programs in the United States and Canada. This edition provides current facts about programs and degrees offered, admission requirements, application information, financial aid, tuition, and housing.

Publication Manual of the American Psychological Association, Fourth Edition, 1994. This new edition, the first revision since the 1983 edition, offers updated information in four key areas: reporting statistics, writing without bias, preparing manuscripts with a word processor for electronic production, and publishing research in accordance with ethical principles of scientific publishing.

The following books are published by VGM Career Books, a division of The McGraw-Hill Companies. Write to VGM Career Books at 4255 West Touhy Avenue, Lincolnwood, IL, 60712-1975, or call 1-800-323-4900.

Great Jobs for Psychology Majors, by Julie DeGalan and Stephen Lambert.

On the Job: Real People Working in the Helping Professions, by Blythe Camenson.

APA-ACCREDITED DOCTORAL PROGRAMS IN PROFESSIONAL PSYCHOLOGY

The Committee on Accreditation of the American Psychological Association approved in 1996 the doctoral programs in clinical, counseling, school, and combined professional-scientific psychology that are conducted by the institutions listed below. In the institutions listed, the approved programs are directed by the department of psychology unless otherwise indicated. Programs that have not requested evaluation and programs that have been evaluated but not approved are not included in the list.

There are three categories of accreditation. Full accreditation is granted to any program that meets the criteria in a satisfactory manner. Provisional accreditation is granted to programs making initial application that do not meet all the criteria but for which the committee believes there is a reasonable expectation that they will be met within a foreseeable period of time. Probation is the category into which a fully accredited program is placed when the committee has evidence that it is not currently in satisfactory compliance with the criteria. (Provisional or probationary accreditation is indicated for any such programs in the following list. All other programs are fully accredited). The criteria for evaluating these programs can be obtained from the Accreditation Office of the American Psychological Association.

Inclusion of an institution in this list indicates approval of doctoral programs in clinical psychology, counseling, school psychology, or combined professional-scientific psychology only. Inclusion or noninclusion carries no implications for other graduate programs in psychology or for programs of graduate education in other disciplines. The first date provided is the original date of accreditation.

CLINICAL PSYCHOLOGY

Adelphi University
    Derner Institute of Advanced
        Psychological Studies
    Garden City, NY 11530
    April 1, 1957
    Next site visit scheduled 2006

Adler School of Professional
        Psychology (Psy.D.)
    Chicago, IL 60601-7203
    November 13, 1998
    Next site visit scheduled 2002

University of Alabama
    Department of Psychology
    Tuscaloosa, AL 35487-0348
    February 1, 1959
    Next site visit scheduled 2000

University of Alabama at
        Birmingham
    Medical Psychology Program
    Birmingham, AL 35294
    March 20, 1985
    Next site visit scheduled 2000

University at Albany/State University
        of New York (formerly listed as
        State University of New York at
        Albany)
    Department of Psychology
    Albany, NY 12222
    May 16, 1979
    Next site visit scheduled 2006

Allegheny University of the Health
        Sciences (formerly listed as
        Hahnemann University and
        Medical College of
        Pennsylvania)
    Department of Clinical and Health
        Psychology
    Philadelphia, PA 19102-1192
    January 15, 1991
    Next site visit scheduled 2003

American School of Professional
        Psychology Hawaii Campus
        (Psy.D.)
    Honolulu, HI 96816
    June 16, 1998
    Next site visit scheduled 2003

American School of Professional
        Psychology Virginia Campus
        (Psy.D.)
    Arlington, VA 22209
    November 30, 1999
    Next site visit scheduled 2002

American University
    Department of Psychology
    Washington, DC 20016
    March 1, 1972
    Next site visit scheduled 2005

Antioch New England Graduate
  School (Psy.D.)
  Department of Clinical
  Psychology
  Keene, NH 03431
  July 15, 1986
  Next site visit scheduled 2005

University of Arizona
  Department of Psychology
  Tucson, AZ 85721
  March 1, 1962
  Next site visit scheduled 2003

Arizona State University
  Department of Psychology
  Tempe, AZ 85287
  January 21, 1977
  Next site visit scheduled 2000

University of Arkansas
  Department of Psychology
  Fayetteville, AR 72701
  April 1, 1966
  Next site visit scheduled 2004

Auburn University
  Department of Psychology
  Auburn University, AL 36849-
  5214
  November 17, 1976
  Next site visit scheduled 2004

Baylor University (Psy.D.)
  Department of Psychology
  Waco, TX 76798-7334
  April 26, 1976
  Next site visit scheduled 2003

Binghamton University/State
  University of New York
  (formerly listed as State
  University of New York at
  Binghamton)
  Department of Psychology
  Binghamton, NY 13902-6000

May 12, 1981
Next site visit scheduled 2003

Biola University (Ph.D., Psy.D.)
  Rosemead School of Psychology
  La Mirada, CA 90639
  May 23, 1980
  Next site visit scheduled 2000

Boston University
  Department of Psychology
  Boston, MA 02215
  October 1, 1948
  Next site visit scheduled 2006

Bowling Green State University
  Department of Psychology
  Bowling Green, OH 43403
  November 1, 1970
  Next site visit scheduled 2003

Brigham Young University
  Department of Psychology
  Provo, UT 84602
  March 1, 1971
  Next site visit scheduled 2004

University of British Columbia
  Department of Psychology
  Vancouver, British Columbia
  Canada V6T 1Y7
  March 25, 1986
  Next self-study review 2001

University at Buffalo/State
  University of New York
  (formerly listed as State
  University of New York at
  Buffalo)
  Department of Psychology
  Buffalo, NY 14260
  November 18, 1949
  Next self-study review 2000

University of California, Berkeley
Department of Psychology
Berkeley, CA 94720-1650
February 1, 1948
Next site visit scheduled 2003

University of California, Los Angeles
Department of Psychology
Los Angeles, CA 90024
February 1, 1948
Next site visit scheduled 2006

California School of Professional
Psychology–Alameda
Alameda, CA 94501
March 21, 1984
Next self-study review 2002

California School of Professional
Psychology–Alameda (Psy.D.)
Alameda, CA 94501
February 28, 1995
Next site visit scheduled 2002

California School of Professional
Psychology–Fresno
Fresno, CA 93727
March 28, 1984
Next site visit scheduled 2000

California School of Professional
Psychology–Fresno (Psy.D.)
Fresno, CA 93727
June 3, 1994
Next site visit scheduled 2003

California School of Professional
Psychology–Los Angeles
Alhambra, CA 91803-1360
March 21, 1978
Next site visit scheduled 2000

California School of Professional
Psychology–Los Angeles
(Psy.D.)
Alhambra, CA 91803-1360

April 23, 1991
Next site visit scheduled 2001

California School of Professional
Psychology–San Diego
San Diego, CA 92121
May 6, 1980
Next site visit scheduled 2000

California School of Professional
Psychology–San Diego (Psy.D.)
San Diego, CA 92121
May 26, 1994
Next site visit scheduled 2000

Carlos Albizu University Miami
Campus (Psy.D.) (formerly
listed as Caribbean Center for
Advanced Studies–Miami
Institute of Psychology)
Professional School of Psychology
Miami, FL 33166
November 21, 1991
Next site visit scheduled 2000

Carlos Albizu University San Juan
Campus (formerly listed as
Caribbean Center for Advanced
Studies)
San Juan, Puerto Rico 00902-3711
September 23, 1994
Next site visit not yet scheduled

Carlos Albizu University San Juan
Campus (Psy.D.) (formerly
listed as Caribbean Center for
Advanced Studies)
San Juan, Puerto Rico 00902-3711
September 23, 1994
Next self-study review 2001

Case Western Reserve University
Department of Psychology
Cleveland, OH 44106
February 1, 1948
Next site visit scheduled 2000

Catholic University of America
   Department of Psychology
   Washington, DC 20064
   February 1, 1948
   Next site visit scheduled 2005

Central Michigan University (Psy.D.)
   Department of Psychology
   Mt. Pleasant, MI 48859
   February 9, 1990
   Next self-study review 2000

Chicago School of Professional
      Psychology (Psy.D.)
   Chicago, IL 60605
   October 6, 1987
   Next site visit scheduled 2002

University of Cincinnati
   Department of Psychology
   Cincinnati, OH 45221-0034
   February 1, 1948
   Next site visit scheduled 2000

City University of New York at City
      College
   Department of Psychology
   New York, NY 10038
   December 1, 1968
   Accredited, on probation
   Next site visit scheduled 2001

Clark University
   Department of Psychology
   Worcester, MA 01610
   February 1, 1948
   Next site visit scheduled 2000

University of Colorado at Boulder
   Department of Psychology
   Boulder, CO 80309
   January 12, 1949
   Next site visit scheduled 2000

Concordia University
   Center for Research in Human
      Development
   Montreal, Quebec
   Canada H3G 1M8
   April 1, 1984
   Next site visit scheduled 2004

University of Connecticut
   Department of Psychology, U-20
   Storrs, CT 06269-1020
   December 19, 1951
   Next site visit scheduled 2003

Dalhousie University
   Department of Psychology
   Halifax, Nova Scotia
   Canada B3H 4J1
   January 16, 1996
   Next site visit scheduled 2001

University of Delaware
   Department of Psychology
   Newark, DE 19716
   November 1, 1971
   Next site visit scheduled 2000

University of Denver
   Department of Psychology
   Denver, CO 80208
   March 27, 1964
   Next site visit scheduled 2006

University of Denver (Psy.D.)
   Graduate School of Professional
      Psychology
   Denver, CO 80208-0208
   May 15, 1979
   Next site visit scheduled 2006

DePaul University
   Department of Psychology
   Chicago, IL 60614
   May 11, 1976
   Next site visit scheduled 2003

University of Detroit Mercy
Department of Psychology
Detroit, MI 48219-0900
June 3, 1988
Accredited, on probation
Next site visit scheduled 2000

Drexel University
Department of Psychology,
Sociology, and Anthropology
Philadelphia, PA 19104
January 31, 1997
Next self-study review 2000

Duke University
Department of Psychology
Durham, NC 27708-0085
February 23, 1948
Next site visit scheduled 2006

Emory University
Department of Psychology
Atlanta, GA 30322
March 1, 1968
Next site visit scheduled 2000

Fairleigh Dickinson University
School of Psychology
Teaneck-Hackensack Campus
Teaneck, NJ 07666
October 21, 1986
Next site visit scheduled 2004

The Fielding Institute
Department of Psychology
Santa Barbara, CA 93105
July 17, 1991
Next site visit scheduled 2003

Finch University of Health Sciences/
Chicago Medical School
(formerly listed as University of
Health Sciences/Chicago
Medical School)
Department of Psychology
North Chicago, IL 60064

October 28, 1983
Next site visit scheduled 2002

University of Florida
Department of Clinical and Health
Psychology
Gainesville, FL 32610
January 1, 1953
Next site visit scheduled 2000

Florida Institute of Technology
(Psy.D.)
School of Psychology
Melbourne, FL 32901-6988
April 26, 1983
Next site visit scheduled 2003

Florida State University
Department of Psychology
Tallahassee, FL 32306-1051
January 1, 1954
Next site visit scheduled 2000

Fordham University
Department of Psychology
Bronx, NY 10458
February 26, 1948
Next site visit scheduled 2000

Forest Institute of Professional
Psychology (Psy.D.)
Springfield, MO 65807
October 14, 1994
Next site visit not yet scheduled

Fuller Theological Seminary
Graduate School of Psychology
Pasadena, CA 91101
December 5, 1972
Next site visit scheduled 2006

Fuller Theological Seminary (Psy.D.)
Graduate School of Psychology
Pasadena, CA 91101
December 5, 1972
Next site visit scheduled 2006

Gallaudet University
Department of Psychology
Washington, DC 20002-3695
October 20, 1995
Next site visit scheduled 2000

George Fox University (Psy.D.)
Graduate School of Clinical
Psychology
Newberg, OR 97132-2697
August 21, 1998
Next site visit scheduled 2003

George Mason University
Department of Psychology
Fairfax, VA 22030-4444
May 15, 1987
Next site visit scheduled 2000

George Washington University
Department of Psychology
Washington, DC 20052
April 1, 1970
Next self-study review 2000

University of Georgia
Department of Psychology
Athens, GA 30602
January 14, 1966
Next site visit scheduled 2004

Georgia School of Professional
Psychology (Psy.D.)
Atlanta, GA 30328
April 28, 1994
Next site visit scheduled 2004

Georgia State University
Department of Psychology
Atlanta, GA 30303-3083
November 28, 1973
Next site visit scheduled 2004

University of Hartford (Psy.D.)
Graduate Institute of Professional
Psychology
Hartford, CT 06105

March 5, 1991
Next site visit scheduled 2000

University of Hawaii at Manoa
Department of Psychology
Honolulu, HI 96822
March 1, 1972
Next site visit scheduled 2000

University of Houston
Department of Psychology
Houston, TX 77204-5341
January 1, 1959
Next site visit scheduled 2006

Howard University
Department of Psychology
Washington, DC 20059
April 7, 1987
Next site visit scheduled 2003

University of Illinois at Chicago
Department of Psychology
Chicago, IL 60680
March 1, 1972
Next site visit scheduled 2000

University of Illinois at Urbana-
Champaign
Department of Psychology
Urbana, IL 61801
February 1, 1948
Next site visit scheduled 2004

Illinois Institute of Technology
Department of Psychology
Chicago, IL 60616
April 30, 1982
Next self-study review 2001

Illinois School of Professional
Psychology Chicago (Psy.D.)
Chicago, IL 60603
February 19, 1985
Next site visit scheduled 2003

Illinois School of Professional
    Psychology Rolling Meadows
    (Psy.D.)
Rolling Meadows, IL 60008
February 26, 1999
Next site visit scheduled 2002

Immaculata College (Psy.D.)
Department of Graduate
    Psychology
Immaculata, PA 19345-0500
April 29, 1999
Next site visit scheduled 2004

Indiana State University (Psy.D.)
Department of Psychology
Terre Haute, IN 47809
June 21, 1985
Next site visit scheduled 2004

Indiana University
Department of Psychology
Bloomington, IN 47405
February 1, 1948
Next site visit scheduled 2003

Indiana University of Pennsylvania
    (Psy.D.)
Department of Psychology
Indiana, PA 15705
November 3, 1987
Next site visit scheduled 2003

Indiana University–Purdue
    University Indianapolis
Department of Psychology
Indianapolis, IN 46202-3275
December 6, 1996
Next self-study review 2001

University of Iowa
Department of Psychology
Iowa City, IA 52242
February 7, 1948
Next site visit scheduled 2003

University of Kansas
Department of Psychology
Lawrence, KS 66045
January 9, 1949
Next site visit scheduled 2000

Kent State University
Department of Psychology
Kent, OH 44242
December 1, 1968
Next site visit scheduled 2006

University of Kentucky
Department of Psychology
Lexington, KY 40506-0044
April 1, 1970
Next site visit scheduled 2006

Loma Linda University
Department of Psychology
Loma Linda, CA 92350
November 13, 1998
Next site visit scheduled 2001

Loma Linda University (Psy.D.)
Department of Psychology
Loma Linda, CA 92350
November 13, 1998
Next site visit scheduled 2003

Long Island University
Department of Psychology
Brooklyn, NY 11201
April 1, 1974
Next site visit scheduled 2000

Long Island University/C. W. Post
    Campus (Psy.D.)
Department of Psychology
Brookville, NY 11548
May 10, 1994
Next site visit scheduled 2004

Louisiana State University
Department of Psychology
Baton Rouge, LA 70803
February 24, 1956
Next self-study review 2001

University of Louisville
Department of Psychology
Louisville, KY 40292
January 19, 1973
Next site visit scheduled 2001

Loyola University of Chicago
Department of Psychology
Chicago, IL 60626
April 2, 1959
Next site visit scheduled 2003

University of Maine
Department of Psychology
Orono, ME 04469-5742
March 1, 1975
Next site visit scheduled 2000

University of Manitoba
Department of Psychology
Winnipeg, Manitoba
Canada R3T 2N2
October 6, 1972
Next self-study review 2000

University of Maryland College Park
Department of Psychology
College Park, MD 20742
October 1, 1963
Next site visit scheduled 2001

University of Maryland Baltimore
County
Department of Psychology
Baltimore, MD 21228
February 9, 1990
Next site visit scheduled 2003

University of Massachusetts at
Amherst
Department of Psychology
Amherst, MA 01003-0034
December 18, 1957
Next site visit scheduled 2000

University of Massachusetts at
Boston
Department of Psychology
Boston, MA 02125-3393
October 1, 1993
Next site visit scheduled 2000

Massachusetts School of Professional
Psychology, Inc. (Psy.D.)
Boston, MA 02132
November 10, 1987
Next site visit scheduled 2000

McGill University
Department of Psychology
Montreal, Quebec
Canada H3A 1B1
April 1, 1968
Next site visit scheduled 2000

The University of Memphis
(formerly listed as Memphis
State University)
Department of Psychology
Memphis, TN 38152
March 1, 1972
Next site visit scheduled 2004

Miami University
Department of Psychology
Oxford, OH 45056
February 1, 1972
Next site visit scheduled 2006

University of Miami
    Department of Psychology
    Coral Gables, FL 33124-8185
    December 1, 1966
    Next site visit scheduled 2000

University of Michigan
    Department of Psychology
    Ann Arbor, MI 48109-1346
    March 2, 1948
    Next site visit scheduled 2006

Michigan State University
    Department of Psychology
    East Lansing, MI 48824-1117
    March 2, 1948
    Next site visit scheduled 2000

University of Minnesota
    Department of Psychology
    Minneapolis, MN 55455-0344
    February 13, 1948
    Next site visit scheduled 2000

Minnesota School of Professional
    Psychology (Psy.D.)
    Bloomington, MN 55437
    January 5, 1993
    Next site visit scheduled 2006

University of Mississippi
    Department of Psychology
    University, MS 38677
    November 6, 1973
    Next self-study review 2000

University of Missouri-Columbia
    Department of Psychology
    Columbia, MO 65211
    January 24, 1958
    Next site visit scheduled 2000

University of Missouri–St. Louis
    Department of Psychology
    St. Louis, MO 63121
    May 3, 1977
    Next site visit scheduled 2006

University of Montana
    Department of Psychology
    Missoula, MT 59812
    March 13, 1970
    Next site visit scheduled 2003

University of Nebraska–Lincoln
    Department of Psychology
    Lincoln, NE 68588-0308
    December 14, 1948
    Next site visit scheduled 2005

University of Nevada, Reno
    Department of Psychology
    Reno, NV 89557
    March 1, 1972
    Next site visit scheduled 2000

University of New Mexico
    Department of Psychology
    Albuquerque, NM 87131
    November 20, 1973
    Next site visit scheduled 2004

The New School for Social Research
    Department of Psychology
    New York, NY 10003
    June 2, 1981
    Next site visit scheduled 2006

New York University
    Department of Psychology
    New York, NY 10003
    February 24, 1948
    Next site visit scheduled 2001

University of North Carolina at
    Chapel Hill
    Department of Psychology
    Chapel Hill, NC 27599-3270
    February 12, 1949
    Next site visit scheduled 2006

University of North Carolina at
    Greensboro
    Department of Psychology
    Greensboro, NC 27412-5001

July 10, 1981
Next site visit scheduled 2004

University of North Dakota
Department of Psychology
Grand Forks, ND 58202-8380
November 1, 1969
Next self-study review 2002

University of North Texas
Department of Psychology
Denton, TX 76203
December 5, 1978
Next site visit scheduled 2002

Northern Illinois University
Department of Psychology
DeKalb, IL 60115
April 1, 1972
Next site visit scheduled 2004

Northwestern University
Department of Psychology
Evanston, IL 60208-2710
May 16, 1986
Next site visit scheduled 2004

Northwestern University Medical
School
Department of Psychiatry and
Behavioral Sciences
Division of Psychology
Chicago, IL 60611
March 1, 1972
Next site visit scheduled 2003

Nova Southeastern University
Center for Psychological Studies
Fort Lauderdale, FL 33314
October 30, 1981
Next site visit scheduled 2000

Nova Southeastern University
(Psy.D.)
Center for Psychological Studies
Fort Lauderdale, FL 33314
March 15, 1983
Next site visit scheduled 2000

Ohio State University
Department of Psychology
Columbus, OH 43210-1222
February 27, 1948
Next site visit scheduled 2000

Ohio University
Department of Psychology
Athens, OH 45701-2979
April 11, 1968
Next site visit scheduled 2003

Oklahoma State University
Department of Psychology
Stillwater, OK 74078
February 1, 1971
Next site visit scheduled 2004

University of Oregon
Department of Psychology
Eugene, OR 97403-1227
March 20, 1958
Next site visit scheduled 2003

University of Ottawa
School of Psychology
Ottawa, Ontario
Canada K1N 6N5
November 22, 1985
Next site visit scheduled 2002

Pacific Graduate School of
Psychology
Palo Alto, CA 94303-4233
March 17, 1988
Next site visit scheduled 2002

Pacific University (Psy.D.)
School of Professional Psychology
Forest Grove, OR 97116
April 3, 1990
Next site visit scheduled 2005

University of Pennsylvania
Department of Psychology
Philadelphia, PA 19104
February 7, 1948
Next site visit scheduled 2005

Pennsylvania State University
Department of Psychology
University Park, PA 16802
February 24, 1948
Next site visit scheduled 2000

Pepperdine University (Psy.D.)
Department of Psychology
Culver City, CA 90230
June 21, 1990
Next site visit scheduled 2005

University of Pittsburgh
Department of Psychology
Pittsburgh, PA 15260
February 20, 1948
Next site visit scheduled 2000

Purdue University
Department of Psychological
Sciences
West Lafayette, IN 47907
February 26, 1948
Next site visit scheduled 2000

Queen's University
Department of Psychology
Kingston, Ontario
Canada K7L 3N6
June 17, 1992
Next site visit scheduled 2000

University of Rhode Island
Department of Psychology
Kingston, RI 02881
April 1, 1972
Next site visit scheduled 2004

University of Rochester
Department of Clinical and Social
Sciences in Psychology
Rochester, NY 14627
March 2, 1948
Next site visit scheduled 2004

Rutgers, The State University of New
Jersey
Department of Psychology
Graduate School of Arts and
Sciences
Busch Campus
Piscataway, NJ 08855
January 8, 1965
Next site visit scheduled 2004

Rutgers, The State University of New
Jersey (Psy.D.)
Department of Clinical
Psychology
Graduate School of Applied and
Professional Psychology
Piscataway, NJ 08854-8085
April 1, 1977
Next site visit scheduled 2004

San Diego State University/
University of California, San
Diego
Joint doctoral program in clinical
psychology
San Diego, CA 92182-4913
June 26, 1990
Next site visit scheduled 2000

University of Saskatchewan
Department of Psychology
Saskatoon, Saskatchewan
Canada S7N 5A5
May 18, 1990
Next site visit scheduled 2003

Simon Fraser University
Psychology Department
Burnaby, British Columbia
Canada V5A 1S6
March 28, 1985
Next site visit scheduled 2003

University of South Carolina
  Department of Psychology
  Columbia, SC 29208-0182
  October 1, 1969
  Next self-study review 2001

University of South Dakota
  Department of Psychology
  Vermillion, SD 57069
  November 1, 1971
  Next site visit scheduled 2004

University of South Florida
  Department of Psychology
  Tampa, FL 33620
  November 1, 1975
  Next site visit scheduled 2003

University of Southern California
  Department of Psychology
  Los Angeles, CA 90089-1061
  February 20, 1948
  Next site visit scheduled 2003

Southern Illinois University
  Department of Psychology
  Carbondale, IL 62901-6502
  December 1, 1961
  Next site visit scheduled 2005

University of Southern Mississippi
  Department of Psychology
  Hattiesburg, MS 39406-0036
  April 27, 1979
  Next self-study review 2000

Spalding University (Psy.D.)
  Department of Psychology
  Louisville, KY 40203
  June 20, 1989
  Next self-study review 2002

St. John's University
  Department of Psychology
  Jamaica, NY 11439
  October 30, 1984
  Next site visit scheduled 2003

St. Louis University
  Department of Psychology
  St. Louis, MO 63103
  May 22, 1964
  Next site visit scheduled 2006

Stony Brook University/State
    University of New York
    (formerly listed as State
    University of New York at
    Stony Brook)
  Department of Psychology
  Stony Brook, NY 11794-2500
  November 1, 1970
  Next site visit scheduled 2006

Syracuse University
  Department of Psychology
  Syracuse, NY 13244-2340
  October 30, 1956
  Next site visit scheduled 2000

Teachers College, Columbia
    University
  Department of Counseling and
    Clinical Psychology
  New York, NY 10027
  February 27, 1948
  Accredited, on probation
  Next site visit scheduled 2001

Temple University
  Department of Psychology
  Philadelphia, PA 19122
  March 18, 1958
  Next site visit scheduled 2004

University of Tennessee, Knoxville
  Department of Psychology
  Knoxville, TN 37996-0900
  February 9, 1949
  Next site visit scheduled 2002

Texas A&M University
  Department of Psychology
  College Station, TX 77843-4235
  April 8, 1988
  Next self-study review 2001

University of Texas at Austin
Department of Psychology
Austin, TX 78712-7789
February 1, 1949
Next site visit scheduled 2006

University of Texas Southwestern
Medical Center at Dallas
Division of Psychology
Dallas, TX 75235-9044
January 17, 1986
Next site visit scheduled 2004

Texas Tech University
Department of Psychology
Lubbock, TX 79409-2051
March 1, 1972
Next site visit scheduled 2001

University of Toledo
Department of Psychology
Toledo, OH 43606
June 1, 1979
Next site visit scheduled 2003

University of Tulsa
Department of Psychology
Tulsa, OK 74104
January 18, 1991
Next self-study review 2002

Uniformed Services University of the
Health Sciences
Department of Medical and
Clinical Psychology
Bethesda, MD 20814-4799
October 23, 1997
Next self-study review 2000

University of Utah
Department of Psychology
Salt Lake City, UT 84112
December 8, 1954
Next site visit scheduled 2000

Vanderbilt University
Department of Psychology
Nashville, TN 37240
February 22, 1952
Next site visit scheduled 2005

Vanderbilt University
Department of Psychology and
Human Development
George Peabody College for
Teachers
Nashville, TN 37240
April 1, 1959
Next site visit scheduled 2004

University of Vermont
Department of Psychology
Burlington, VT 05405
November 12, 1973
Next site visit scheduled 2003

University of Victoria
Department of Psychology
Victoria, British Columbia
Canada V8W 3P5
January 12, 1993
Next self-study review 2002

University of Virginia
Department of Human Services
Curry School of Education
Charlottesville, VA 22903-2495
November 4, 1988
Next site visit scheduled 2006

University of Virginia
Department of Psychology
Charlottesville, VA 22903
October 25, 1988
Next site visit scheduled 2004

(The doctoral programs in clinical
psychology at the University of
Virginia were formerly part of a
single program at the Institute of
Clinical Psychology cosponsored by

the Curry School of Education and the Department of Psychology, College of Arts and Sciences. They are now separate programs.)

Virginia Commonwealth University
Department of Psychology
Richmond, VA 23284-2018
April 1, 1975
Next site visit scheduled 2004

Virginia Consortium for Professional
Psychology (Psy.D.)
Virginia Beach, VA 23452
December 16, 1982
Next site visit scheduled 2006

Virginia Polytechnic Institute and
State University
Department of Psychology
Blacksburg, VA 24061-0436
April 17, 1980
Next site visit scheduled 2000

University of Washington
Department of Psychology
Seattle, WA 98195
March 3, 1948
Next site visit scheduled 2003

Washington State University
Department of Psychology
Pullman, WA 99164-4820
February 14, 1956
Next site visit scheduled 2005

Washington University
Department of Psychology
St. Louis, MO 63130
February 20, 1948
Next site visit scheduled 2004

University of Waterloo
Department of Psychology
Waterloo, Ontario
Canada N2L 3G1
March 1, 1970
Next site visit scheduled 2002

Wayne State University
Department of Psychology
Detroit, MI 48202
August 1, 1960
Next site visit scheduled 2004

West Virginia University
Department of Psychology
Morgantown, WV 26506-6040
January 1, 1966
Next site visit scheduled 2005

Western Michigan University
Department of Psychology
Kalamazoo, MI 49008
April 16, 1991
Next site visit scheduled 2006

University of Western Ontario
Department of Psychology
London, Ontario
Canada N6A 5C2
September 26, 1986
Next site visit scheduled 2000

Wheaton College (Psy.D.)
Department of Psychology
Wheaton, IL 60187-5593
May 1, 1998
Next self-study review 2001

Widener University (Psy.D.)
Department of Psychology
Institute for Graduate Clinical
Psychology
Chester, PA 19013
July 1, 1989
Next site visit scheduled 2000

University of Windsor
Department of Psychology
Windsor, Ontario
Canada N9B 3P4
July 26, 1988
Next site visit scheduled 2000

University of Wisconsin–Madison
Department of Psychology
Madison, WI 53706
February 12, 1948
Next site visit scheduled 2000

University of Wisconsin–Milwaukee
Department of Psychology
Milwaukee, WI 53201
October 14, 1980
Next self-study review 2002

The Wright Institute (Psy.D.)
Department of Psychology
Berkeley, CA 94704
March 10, 1998
Next site visit scheduled 2005

Wright State University (Psy.D.)
School of Professional Psychology
Dayton, OH 45435
March 16, 1982
Next site visit scheduled 2004

University of Wyoming
Department of Psychology
Laramie, WY 82071
December 8, 1972
Next site visit scheduled 2003

Yale University
Department of Psychology
New Haven, CT 06520-8205

February 1, 1948
Next site visit scheduled 2000

Yeshiva University (Psy.D.)
Ferkauf Graduate School of
Psychology
Albert Einstein College of
Medicine Campus
Bronx, NY 10461
November 7, 1985
Next site visit scheduled 2003

York University
Department of Psychology
Toronto, Ontario
Canada M3J 1P3
March 31, 1994
Next site visit scheduled 2002

York University
Department of Psychology
Toronto, Ontario
Canada M3J 1P3
May 28, 1999
Next site visit scheduled 2004

(This program in clinical psychology
is separate from the other accredited
program in clinical psychology in
York University's Department of
Psychology. That program provides
training in clinical psychology with a
developmental emphasis.)

COUNSELING PSYCHOLOGY

The University of Akron
Department of Psychology
Department of Counseling and
Special Education
Akron, OH 44325
April 13, 1990
Next site visit scheduled 2005

University at Albany/State University
of New York (formerly listed as

State University of New York at
Albany)
Department of Educational and
Counseling Psychology
Division of Counseling
Psychology
Albany, NY 12222
May 8, 1980
Next site visit scheduled 2005

Arizona State University
Division of Psychology and
Education
Tempe, AZ 85287-0611
April 1, 1972
Next site visit scheduled 2006

Auburn University
Department of Counseling and
Counseling Psychology
Auburn University, AL 36849
May 6, 1988
Next site visit scheduled 2003

Ball State University
Department of Counseling
Psychology and Guidance
Services
Muncie, IN 47306
May 4, 1982
Next site visit scheduled 2005

Boston College
Department of Counseling,
Developmental, and
Educational Psychology
Chestnut Hill, MA 02167
May 7, 1982
Next site visit scheduled 2000

Boston University (Ed.D.)
Department of Developmental
Studies and Counseling
Boston, MA 02215
May 11, 1982

(This program is no longer admitting
students and is scheduled to be
phased out.)

University of California, Santa
Barbara
Department of Education
Santa Barbara, CA 93106
May 1, 1981

(This program is no longer admitting
students and is scheduled to be
phased out. The program is being
replaced by an accredited program in
combined professional-scientific
psychology.)

Colorado State University
Department of Psychology
Fort Collins, CO 80523
March 1, 1970
Next site visit scheduled 2000

University of Denver
School of Education
Denver, CO 80208
May 16, 1986
Next site visit scheduled 2000

University of Florida
Department of Psychology
Gainesville, FL 32611-2250
January 15, 1954
Next site visit scheduled 2003

Fordham University
Division of Psychological and
Educational Services
New York, NY 10023
April 19, 1990
Next site visit scheduled 2003

University of Georgia
Department of Counseling
Psychology
Athens, GA 30602
April 3, 1984
Next site visit scheduled 2003

Georgia State University
Department of Counseling and
Psychological Services
Atlanta, GA 30303
May 1, 1984
Next site visit scheduled 2006

University of Houston
  Department of Educational
    Psychology
  Houston, TX 77204-5874
  April 14, 1987
  Next site visit scheduled 2003

University of Illinois
    at Urbana–Champaign
  Department of Educational
    Psychology
  Champaign, IL 61820
  November 8, 1985
  Next site visit scheduled 2000

Indiana State University
  Department of Counseling
  Terre Haute, IN 47809
  May 6, 1980
  Next site visit scheduled 2000

Indiana University
  Department of Counseling and
    Educational Psychology
  Bloomington, IN 47405-1006
  June 23, 1988
  Next site visit scheduled 2003

University of Iowa
  Division of Psychological and
    Quantitative Foundations
  Iowa City, IA 52242-1316
  May 13, 1980
  Next site visit scheduled 2005

Iowa State University
  Department of Psychology
  Ames, IA 50011-3180
  March 1, 1973
  Next site visit scheduled 2003

University of Kansas
  Department of Psychology and
    Research in Education
  Lawrence, KS 66045-2338
  March 1, 1971
  Next site visit scheduled 2001

Kent State University
  College of Education
  Kent, OH 44242
  March 14, 1989
  Accredited, on probation

(This program is no longer admitting students and is scheduled to be phased out.)

University of Kentucky
  Department of Educational and
    Counseling Psychology
  Lexington, KY 40506-0017
  November 9, 1983
  Next site visit scheduled 2004

Lehigh University
  Counseling Psychology, School
    Psychology, and Special
    Education
  Bethlehem, PA 18015-4792
  December 3, 1993
  Next self-study review 2001

University of Louisville
  Department of Educational and
    Counseling Psychology
  Louisville, KY 40292
  November 18, 1999
  Next site visit scheduled 2004

✳ Loyola University of Chicago
  Department of Counseling
    Psychology
  Chicago, IL 60091
  November 29, 1984
  Next site visit scheduled 2003

University of Maryland College Park
  Department of Counseling and
    Personnel Services/Department
    of Psychology
  College Park, MD 20742
  April 16, 1953
  Next site visit scheduled 2004

The University of Memphis
(formerly listed as Memphis
State University)
Department of Counseling,
Educational Psychology, and
Research
Memphis, TN 38152
October 17, 1989
Next site visit scheduled 2005

✳ University of Miami
Department of Educational and
Psychological Studies
Coral Gables, FL 33124
February 7, 1989
Next site visit scheduled 2000

Michigan State University
Department of Counseling,
Educational Psychology, and
Special Education
East Lansing, MI 48824
April 8, 1977
Next site visit scheduled 2004

University of Minnesota
Counseling and Personnel
Psychology Program
Department of Educational
Psychology
Minneapolis, MN 55455
April 8, 1965
Next site visit scheduled 2001

University of Minnesota
Department of Psychology
Minneapolis, MN 55455
December 15, 1952
Next site visit scheduled 2003

University of Missouri–Columbia
Department of Educational and
Counseling Psychology and
Department of Psychology
Columbia, MO 65211

April 29, 1953
Next site visit scheduled 2004

University of Missouri–Kansas City
Division of Counseling
Psychology and Counselor
Education
Kansas City, MO 64110
February 22, 1985
Next site visit scheduled 2003

University of Nebraska–Lincoln
Department of Educational
Psychology
Lincoln, NE 68588-0345
April 20, 1959
Next site visit scheduled 2000

New Mexico State University
Department of Counseling and
Educational Psychology
Las Cruces, NM 88003-0001
May 2, 1995
Next site visit scheduled 2005

✳ New York University
Department of Applied
Psychology
New York, NY 10003
April 17, 1981
Next self-study review 2000

University of North Dakota
Department of Counseling
Grand Forks, ND 58202-8255
April 10, 1987
Next site visit scheduled 2000

University of North Texas
Department of Psychology
Denton, TX 76203-3587
December 5, 1978
Next site visit scheduled 2003

University of Northern Colorado
Division of Professional
Psychology
Greeley, CO 80639
April 4, 1995
Next site visit scheduled 2003

Northwestern University
Department of Counseling
Psychology
Evanston, IL 60208
March 3, 1988

(This program is no longer admitting students and is scheduled to be phased out.)

University of Notre Dame
Department of Psychology
Notre Dame, IN 46556
March 1, 1972
Next site visit scheduled 2005

Ohio State University
Department of Psychology
Columbus, OH 43210-1222
December 15, 1952
Next site visit scheduled 2004

University of Oklahoma
Department of Educational
Psychology
Norman, OK 73019-0260
October 25, 1988
Next site visit scheduled 2006

Oklahoma State University
Applied Behavioral Studies in
Education
Stillwater, OK 74078
November 20, 1992
Next site visit scheduled 2003

University of Oregon
Department of Applied Behavioral
and Communication Sciences
Eugene, OR 97403-5251

January 12, 1955
Next site visit scheduled 2001

Our Lady of the Lake University
(Psy.D.)
School of Education and Clinical
Studies
San Antonio, TX 78207-4689
May 12, 1995
Next site visit scheduled 2003

Pennsylvania State University
Division of Counselor Education,
Counseling Psychology, and
Rehabilitation Services
University Park, PA 16802
November 12, 1982
Next site visit scheduled 2006

University of Pittsburgh
Psychology in Education
Pittsburgh, PA 15260
April 13, 1990
Next site visit scheduled 2002

(This program is no longer admitting students and is scheduled to be phased out.)

University of San Francisco (Psy.D.)
Department of Counseling
Psychology
San Francisco, CA 94117-1080
April 22, 1994
Accredited, on probation
Next site visit scheduled 2003

(This program is no longer admitting students and is scheduled to be phased out.)

Seton Hall University
Department of Professional
Psychology and Family
Therapy
South Orange, NJ 07079-2685
October 22, 1999
Next site visit scheduled 2006

University of Southern California
Division of Counseling and
Educational Psychology
Los Angeles, CA 90089-0031
March 19, 1993
Next site visit scheduled 2003

⅄ Southern Illinois University
Department of Psychology
Carbondale, IL 62901
December 1, 1961
Next site visit scheduled 2000

University of Southern Mississippi
Department of Psychology
Hattiesburg, MS 39406-5012
June 29, 1979
Next site visit not yet scheduled

Stanford University
School of Education
Stanford, CA 94305
April 19, 1985
Next site visit scheduled 2003

✳ Teachers College, Columbia
University (Ph.D., Ed.D.)
Department of Counseling and
Clinical Psychology
New York, NY 10027
January 1, 1952
Next self-study review 2000

Temple University
Department of Psychological
Studies in Education
Philadelphia, PA 19122
January 30, 1973
Next site visit scheduled 2001

University of Tennessee, Knoxville
Department of Counseling,
Deafness, and Human Services
Knoxville, TN 37996
April 18, 1980
Next site visit not yet scheduled

Texas A&M University
Department of Educational
Psychology
College Station, TX 77843-4225
December 8, 1981
Next site visit scheduled 2003

✳ University of Texas at Austin
Department of Educational
Psychology
Austin, TX 78712
January 12, 1953
Next site visit not yet scheduled

Texas Tech University
Department of Psychology
Lubbock, TX 79409
April 24, 1964
Next site visit scheduled 2006

Texas Woman's University
Department of Psychology and
Philosophy
Denton, TX 76204
June 20, 1995
Next site visit scheduled 2005

University of Utah
Department of Educational
Psychology
Salt Lake City, UT 84112
March 1, 1957
Next site visit scheduled 2006

Virginia Commonwealth University
Department of Psychology
Richmond, VA 23284-2018
October 28, 1980
Next site visit scheduled 2006

Washington State University
Department of Educational
Leadership and Counseling
Psychology
Pullman, WA 99164-2136
September 29, 1989
Next site visit scheduled 2000

West Virginia University
  Department of Counseling,
    Rehabilitation Counseling, and
    Counseling Psychology
  Morgantown, WV 26506-6122
  January 13, 1989
  Next site visit scheduled 2005

Western Michigan University
  Department of Counselor
    Education and Counseling
    Psychology
  Kalamazoo, MI 49008
  February 12, 1993
  Next site visit scheduled 2005

University of Wisconsin–Madison
  Department of Counseling
    Psychology
  Madison, WI 53706
  October 29, 1985
  Next site visit scheduled 2006

University of Wisconsin–Milwaukee
  Department of Educational
    Psychology
  Milwaukee, WI 53201
  October 14, 1996
  Next self-study review 2001

SCHOOL PSYCHOLOGY

University at Albany/State University
    of New York (Psy.D.) (formerly
    listed as State University of
    New York at Albany)
  School of Education
  Albany, NY 12222
  September 18, 1992
  Next site visit scheduled 2005

University of Arizona
  College of Education
  Tucson, AZ 85721
  October 19, 1979
  Next site visit scheduled 2006

Arizona State University
  College of Education
  Tempe, AZ 85287-0611
  April 30, 1982
  Next site visit scheduled 2005

Ball State University
  Department of Educational
    Psychology
  Muncie, IN 47306
  May 3, 1985
  Next site visit scheduled 2000

University of California, Berkeley
  School of Education
  Berkeley, CA 94720
  November 25, 1980
  Accredited, on probation
  Next site visit not yet scheduled

University of Cincinnati
  School Psychology, Division of
    Human Services
  Cincinnati, OH 45221-0002
  February 9, 1983
  Accredited, on probation
  Next site visit scheduled 2000

University of Florida
  Department of Educational
    Psychology
  Gainesville, FL 32611-7047
  October 28, 1997
  Next site visit scheduled 2000

Fordham University
  Division of Psychological and
    Educational Services
  New York, NY 10023
  October 25, 1983
  Next site visit scheduled 2003

University of Georgia
  Department of Educational
    Psychology
  Athens, GA 30602
  September 27, 1983
  Next site visit scheduled 2005

Georgia State University
  Department of Counseling and
    Psychological Services
  Atlanta, GA 30303
  May 1, 1979
  Next site visit scheduled 2001

Illinois State University
  Department of Psychology
  Normal, IL 61790-4620
  April 7, 1998
  Next self-study review 2001

Indiana University
  School of Education
  Bloomington, IN 47405
  April 20, 1983
  Next site visit scheduled 2005

Indiana State University
  Department of Educational and
    School Psychology
  Terre Haute, IN 47809
  June 20, 1980
  Next site visit scheduled 2001

University of Iowa
  Psychological and Quantitative
    Foundations
  Iowa City, IA 52242
  March 31, 1992
  Next site visit scheduled 2000

University of Kansas
  Department of Psychology and
    Research in Education
  Lawrence, KS 66045
  March 9, 1983
  Next site visit scheduled 2000

Kent State University
  Department of Educational
    Foundations and Special
    Services
  Kent, OH 44242
  May 1, 1984
  Next self-study review 2000

University of Kentucky
  Department of Educational and
    Counseling Psychology
  Lexington, KY 40506-0017
  February 18, 1986
  Next site visit scheduled 2002

Lehigh University
  Department of Education and
    Human Services
  Bethlehem, PA 18015-4792
  October 12, 1990
  Next site visit scheduled 2006

University of Maryland College Park
  Department of Counseling and
    Personnel Services
  College Park, MD 20742-1125
  February 28, 1984
  Next self-study review 2000

University of Massachusetts at
    Amherst
  Department of Student
    Development and Pupil
    Personnel Services
  Amherst, MA 01003
  April 8, 1992
  Next self-study review 2000

McGill University
  Department of Educational and
    Counseling Psychology
  Montreal, Quebec
  Canada H3A 1Y2
  May 22, 1998
  Next site visit scheduled 2001

Michigan State University
 Department of Counseling,
  Educational Psychology, and
  Special Education
 East Lansing, MI 48824
 October 25, 1985
 Next site visit scheduled 2004

University of Minnesota
 College of Education
 Minneapolis, MN 55455
 May 1, 1972
 Next site visit scheduled 2003

Mississippi State University
 Department of Counselor
  Education and Educational
  Psychology
 Mississippi State, MS 39762-5740
 December 10, 1996
 Next site visit scheduled 2003

University of Missouri–Columbia
 Department of Educational and
  Counseling Psychology
 Columbia, MO 65211
 February 5, 1999
 Next site visit scheduled 2004

University of Nebraska–Lincoln
 Department of Educational
  Psychology
 Lincoln, NE 68588
 December 5, 1980
 Next site visit scheduled 2003

New York University
 Department of Applied
  Psychology
 New York, NY 10003-6674
 April 13, 1979
 Next self-study review 2000

New York University (Psy.D.)
 Department of Applied
  Psychology

New York, NY 10003-6674
 April 26, 1985
 Next site visit scheduled 2006

University of North Carolina at
  Chapel Hill
 Division of Organizational and
  Psychological Studies
 Chapel Hill, NC 27599-3500
 June 5, 1979
 Next site visit scheduled 2004

North Carolina State University
 Department of Psychology
 Raleigh, NC 27695-7801
 April 10, 1987
 Next site visit scheduled 2000

University of Northern Colorado
 Division of Professional
  Psychology
 Greeley, CO 80639
 June 25, 1981
 Next site visit scheduled 2000

Oklahoma State University
 School of Applied Health and
  Educational Psychology
 Stillwater, OK 74078
 October 28, 1997
 Next site visit scheduled 2000

University of Oregon
 Department of Special Education
  and Community Resources
 Eugene, OR 97403-5261
 June 1, 1994
 Next site visit scheduled 2006

Pennsylvania State University
 Division of Educational and
  School Psychology and Special
  Education
 University Park, PA 16802
 June 19, 1978
 Next site visit scheduled 2003

University of Rhode Island
Department of Psychology
Kingston, RI 02881
November 1, 1975
Next site visit scheduled 2001

Rutgers, The State University of New
Jersey (Psy.D.)
Department of Applied
Psychology
Graduate School of Applied and
Professional Psychology
Piscataway, NJ 08854-8085
April 1, 1977
Next site visit scheduled 2004

University of South Carolina
Department of Psychology
Columbia, SC 29208
February 1, 1974
Next self-study review 2002

University of South Florida
Department of Psychological and
Social Foundations
Tampa, FL 33620
November 20, 1998
Next site visit scheduled 2003

University of Southern Mississippi
Department of Psychology
Hattiesburg, MS 39406-5025
September 27, 1983
Next site visit scheduled 2003

Syracuse University
Department of Psychology
Syracuse, NY 13244-2340
April 26, 1988
Next site visit scheduled 2000

Teachers College, Columbia
University (Ed.D.)
Department of Health and
Behavior Studies

Program in Applied Educational
Psychology
New York, NY 10027
March 31, 1988
Accredited, on probation
Next site visit scheduled 2000

(This program originally offered both
the Ph.D. and the Ed.D. Currently
only the Ed.D.degree is being
offered.)

Temple University
Department of Psychological
Studies in Education
Philadelphia, PA 19122
April 4, 1978
Next site visit scheduled 2003

University of Tennessee, Knoxville
Psychoeducational Studies
Knoxville, TN 37996
April 23, 1991
Next site visit scheduled 2000

Texas A&M University
Department of Educational
Psychology
College Station, TX 77843
October 29, 1985
Next site visit scheduled 2003

University of Texas at Austin
Department of Educational
Psychology
Austin, TX 78712
February 1, 1971
Next site visit scheduled 2006

Tulane University
Department of Psychology
New Orleans, LA 70118
August 9, 1991
Next site visit scheduled 2000

University of Utah
  Department of Educational
    Psychology
  Salt Lake City, UT 84112
  January 14, 1983
  Next site visit scheduled 2006

University of Washington
  Area of Educational Psychology
  Seattle, WA 98195
  October 25, 1991
  Next site visit scheduled 2000

University of Wisconsin–Madison
  Department of Educational
    Psychology
  Madison, WI 53706

February 27, 1986
Next site visit scheduled 2004

University of Wisconsin–Milwaukee
  Department of Educational
    Psychology
  Milwaukee, WI 53201
  October 14, 1996
  Next self-study review 2001

Yeshiva University (Psy.D.)
  Department of School Psychology
  Ferkauf Graduate School of
    Psychology
  Bronx, NY 10461
  November 7, 1985
  Next site visit not yet scheduled

COMBINED PROFESSIONAL-SCIENTIFIC PSYCHOLOGY

University at Buffalo/State
  University of New York
  (formerly listed as State
  University of New York at
  Buffalo) (counseling/school)
  Department of Counseling and
    Educational Psychology
  Buffalo, NY 14260
  October 6, 1978
  Next site visit scheduled 2002

(This program previously was listed
as an accredited program in
counseling psychology. It has since
incorporated a school component and
is now an accredited program in
combined professional-scientific
psychology.)

University of California, Santa
  Barbara (clinical/counseling/
  school)
  Department of Education
  Santa Barbara, CA 93106

December 7, 1990
Next site visit scheduled 2006

Florida State University (counseling/
  school)
  Department of Human Services
    and Studies
  Tallahassee, FL 32306
  December 8, 1995
  Next site visit scheduled 2002

Hofstra University (clinical/school)
  Department of Psychology
  Hempstead, NY 11550
  October 16, 1973
  Next site visit scheduled 2005

James Madison University (Psy.D.)
  (clinical/counseling/school)
  School of Psychology
  Harrisonburg, VA 22807
  October 29, 1996
  Next self-study review 2000

University of Massachusetts at
Amherst (school/counseling)
School of Education
Amherst, MA 01003
April 8, 1992

(This program is no longer admitting
students and is scheduled to be
phased out.)

Northeastern University (counseling/
school)
Department of Counseling,
Psychology, Rehabilitation, and
Special Education
Bouve College of Pharmacy and
Health Sciences
Boston, MA 02115
October 31, 1995
Next site visit scheduled 2000

Pace University (Psy.D.) (school/
clinical)
Department of Psychology
New York, NY 10038
November 4, 1988
Next site visit scheduled 2006

(This program previously was listed
as an accredited program in school
psychology. It has since incorporated
a clinical component and is now an
accredited program in combined
professional-scientific psychology.)

University of Pennsylvania (clinical/
school)
Psychology in Education Division
Philadelphia, PA 19104

September 27, 1996
Next site visit scheduled 2000

University of Pennsylvania
(counseling/school)
Psychology in Education Division
Philadelphia, PA 19104
February 1, 1981
Accredited, on probation

(This program is no longer admitting
students and is scheduled to be
phased out. Probation status resulting
from the program not admitting
students for two consecutive years.)

Utah State University (clinical/
counseling/school)
Department of Psychology
Logan, UT 84322
February 1, 1975
Next site visit scheduled 2004

Yeshiva University (Psy.D.) (school/
clinical)
Ferkauf Graduate School of
Psychology
Bronx, NY 10461
October 23, 1998
Next site visit scheduled 2003

APPENDIX C

APA-ACCREDITED PREDOCTORAL INTERNSHIPS FOR DOCTORAL TRAINING IN CLINICAL AND COUNSELING PSYCHOLOGY

In 1996, the Committee on Accreditation of the American Psychological Association approved for doctoral training in professional psychology the internships offered on the following pages. There is no longer a distinction, as there once was, between clinical and counseling internship programs.

There are three categories of accreditation. Full accreditation is granted to any program that meets the criteria in a satisfactory manner. Provisional accreditation is granted to programs making initial application that do not meet all the criteria but for which the committee believes there is a reasonable expectation that they will be met within a foreseeable period of time. Probation is the category into which a fully accredited program is placed when the committee has evidence that it is not currently in satisfactory compliance with the criteria. The criteria for evaluating these programs can be obtained from the Accreditation Office of the American Psychological Association.

Alabama
University of Alabama at
  Birmingham Medical Center
Central Alabama Veterans Health
  Care System (formerly listed as
  Veterans Affairs Medical Center)

Arizona
University of Arizona College of
  Medicine
Arizona State University Counseling
  and Consultation
Carl T. Hayden Veterans Affairs
  Medical Center

Phoenix Psychology Internship Consortium c/o Carl T. Hayden Veterans Affairs Medical Center

Southern Arizona Psychology Internship Consortium Veterans Affairs Medical Center

Arkansas

University of Arkansas for Medical Sciences

Arkansas Mental Health Services Division

John L. McClellan Memorial Veterans Hospital

California

Atascadero State Hospital

University of California, Berkeley Counseling and Psychological Services Center

University of California, Davis Counseling Center

University of California, Irvine Counseling Center

University of California, Los Angeles–Student Psychological Services

University of California, Los Angeles School of Medicine

University of California, San Diego Psychological and Counseling Services

University of California, San Diego Psychology Internship Consortium, Department of Psychiatry

University of California, San Francisco School of Medicine

University of California, Santa Barbara Counseling and Career Services (Probation status resulting from the program not having interns in training year 1997–1998.)

University of California, Santa Cruz Counseling and Psychological Services, Cowell Student Health Center

California State University, Long Beach–Counseling and Psychological Services

Central California Psychology Internship Consortium

Child and Family Guidance Center (formerly listed as San Fernando Valley Child Guidance Clinic)

Children's Hospital of Orange County–Health Psychology Department

Didi Hirsch Community Mental Health Center

Greater Long Beach Child Guidance Center, Inc.

The H.E.L.P. Group

Jerry L. Pettis Memorial Veterans Affairs Hospital

Kaiser Permanente Medical Care Program–Department of Psychiatry

Kaiser Permanente Medical Care Program–Department of Psychiatry and Addiction Medicine

The Metropolitan Detention Center–Federal Bureau of Prisons

Napa State Hospital

Naval Medical Center, San Diego

Pacific Clinics

Packard Children's Hospital at Stanford/The Children's Health Council

136   *Opportunities in Psychology Careers*

Patton State Hospital
Richmond Area Multi-Services, Inc.
San Bernardino County Department
    of Mental Health
Sharp HealthCare
Shasta Community Mental Health
    Center
University of Southern California
    Student Counseling Services
St. John's Child and Family
    Development Center (formerly
    listed as St. John's Child Study
    Center)
VA Greater Los Angeles Healthcare
    System (formerly listed as
    Veterans Affairs Medical Center
    and as Veterans Affairs Outpatient
    Clinic)
Veterans Affairs Medical Center
Veterans Affairs Northern California
    Health Care System
Veterans Affairs Palo Alto Health
    Care System (formerly listed as
    Veterans Affairs Medical Center)

Colorado
Adams Community Mental Health
    Center
The Children's Hospital
University of Colorado Health
    Sciences Center
Colorado Mental Health Institute at
    Fort Logan
Colorado State University
    Counseling Center
University of Denver Counseling and
    Behavioral Health
Denver Health Medical Center
    (formerly listed as Denver General
    Hospital)
Veterans Affairs Medical Center

Connecticut
Connecticut Valley Psychology
    Internship Program (formerly
    listed as Connecticut Valley
    Hospital)
Greater Hartford Clinical Psychology
    Internship Consortium
Institute of Living/Hartford
    Hospital's Mental Health Network
VA Connecticut Health Care System
    (formerly listed as Veterans
    Affairs Medical Center)
VA Connecticut Healthcare System-
    Newington
The Village for Families and
    Children, Inc.
Yale Child Study Center
Yale University School of
    Medicine–Department of
    Psychiatry

Delaware
Alfred I. Dupont Institute of the
    Nemours Foundation–Department
    of Pediatrics
University of Delaware Center for
    Counseling and Student
    Development

District of Columbia
Children's National Medical Center
    (formerly listed as Children's
    Hospital, National Medical
    Center)
Georgetown University Child
    Development Center (formerly
    listed as Georgetown University
    Hospital)
George Washington University
    Counseling Center

Government of the District of Columbia–Department of Human Services
Howard University Counseling Service–Division of Student Affairs
Howard University Hospital
Veterans Affairs Medical Center
Walter Reed Army Medical Center–Department of Psychology

Florida
The Children's Psychiatric Center, Inc.
Federal Correctional Institution
University of Florida Counseling Center (formerly listed as University of Florida Psychological and Vocational Counseling Center)
University of Florida Health Science Center (formerly listed as University of Florida–J. Hillis Miller Science Center)
Florida State Hospital
James A. Haley Veterans Affairs Hospital
Mailman Center for Child Development–University of Miami School of Medicine
University of Miami Counseling Center
University of Miami/Jackson Memorial Medical Center
North Florida/South Georgia Veterans Health System (formerly listed as Veterans Affairs Medical Center)
Northwest Dade Center, Inc.

Nova Southeastern University Community Mental Health Center
University of South Florida Counseling Center for Human Development
University of South Florida/Louis de la Parte Florida Mental Health Institute
Veterans Affairs Medical Center

Georgia
Bradley Center of St. Francis (formerly listed as Bradley Center, Inc.)
Dwight D. Eisenhower Army Medical Center
Emory University Counseling Center
Emory University School of Medicine/Grady Health Systems Hospital Department of Psychiatry (Psychology)
University of Georgia Counseling and Testing Center
Georgia State University Counseling Center
Medical College of Georgia/VAMC Psychology Residency (formerly listed as Medical College of Georgia/VAMC Internship Consortium)
U.S. Penitentiary–Atlanta, GA
Veterans Affairs Medical Center (Atlanta)
Veterans Affairs Medical Center–Augusta

Hawaii
University of Hawaii Center for Counseling and Student Development

Tripler Army Medical Center–Clinical Psychology Service
Veterans Affairs Outpatient Clinic

Illinois
Advocate Health Care–Family Care Network–Department of Clinical and Educational Services
Allendale Association
Cermak Health Services of Cook County
University of Chicago Medical Center–Department of Psychiatry
Chicago–Read Mental Health Center
Children's Memorial Hospital Department of Child and Adolescent Psychiatry
University of Illinois at Champaign Counseling Center
University of Illinois at Chicago Counseling Center
University of Illinois at Chicago, Department of Psychiatry/ Psychiatric Institute (formerly listed as Illinois State Psychiatric Institute)
Illinois Masonic Medical Center
Illinois State University Student Counseling Services (formerly listed as Illinois State University Counseling and Career Services)
Institute for Juvenile Research
La Rabida Children's Hospital and Research Center
The Menta Group
Michael Reese Hospital and Medical Center
Northern Illinois University Counseling and Student Development Center

Northwestern University Medical School/Northwestern Memorial Hospital Division of Clinical Psychology
Oak Forest Hospital–Psychology Department
Ravenswood Hospital Community Mental Health Center
Rush-Presbyterian/St. Luke's Medical Center
Southern Illinois University at Carbondale Counseling Center
Turning Point Behavioral Health Care Center
VA-Edward Hines, Jr., Hospital Veterans Affairs Medical Center
West Side Veterans Affairs Medical Center

Indiana
Ball State University Counseling and Psychological Services Center
Butler University/BehaviorCorp (formerly listed as Butler University Counseling Center)
Center for Behavioral Health (formerly listed as South Central Community Mental Health Center, Inc.)
Evansville Psychology Internship Consortium
Hamilton Center, Inc.
Indiana University Health Center–Counseling and Psychological Services
Indiana University School of Medicine
University of Notre Dame Counseling Center (formerly listed as University of Notre Dame Counseling Center/Oaklawn

Psychiatric/Community Mental Health Center) Park Center, Inc.

Quinco Behavioral Health Systems (formerly listed as Quinco Consulting Center, Inc.)

Southlake Center for Mental Health

Tri-City Community Mental Health Center

Iowa

Des Moines Child and Adolescent Guidance Center, Inc. (formerly listed as Des Moines Child Guidance Center, Inc.)

University of Iowa Counseling Service

Iowa State University Student Counseling Service

VA Central Iowa Health Care System, Knoxville Division (formerly listed as Veterans Affairs Medical Center)

Kansas

Colmery-O'Neil Veterans Affairs Medical Center

Dwight D. Eisenhower Veterans Affairs Medical Center

University of Kansas Counseling and Psychological Services

Kansas State University Psychology Internship Program

Wichita Collaborative Psychology Internship Program–Counseling and Testing Center

Kentucky

East Kentucky Rural Psychology Predoctoral Internship–ARH Psychiatric Center

Federal Medical Center

Jefferson County Internship Consortium

University of Louisville School of Medicine

Veterans Affairs Medical Center

Louisiana

Central Louisiana State Hospital

The Louisiana School Psychology Internship Consortium

Louisiana State University School of Medicine

Southern Louisiana Internship Consortium

Tulane Medical School (formerly listed as Tulane University School of Medicine)

Maine

University of Maine Counseling Center

Veterans Affairs Medical Center

Maryland

Baltimore Area VA Residency Training Program (formerly listed as Baltimore Area Veterans Affairs Medical Center)

Crownsville Hospital Center–Department of Health and Mental Hygiene

The Kennedy Krieger Institute–Department of Psychology

Malcolm Grow USAF Medical Center

University of Maryland Counseling Center

University of Maryland School of Medicine–Department of Pediatrics, Division of Behavioral and Developmental Pediatrics

University of Maryland School of Medicine–Department of Psychiatry

National Naval Medical Center–Psychology Department

Regional Institute for Children and Adolescents

Spring Grove Hospital Center

Springfield Hospital Center

Towson University Counseling Center (formerly listed as Towson State University Counseling Center)

VA Maryland Health Care System–Perry Point Division (formerly listed as Veterans Affairs Medical Center)

Massachusetts

Beth Israel Hospital–Department of Psychiatry

Boston Consortium in Clinical Psychology (formerly listed as Tufts University School of Medicine/Boston Veterans Affairs Psychology Internship Consortium)

Boston Medical Center (formerly listed as Boston City Hospital)–Center for Multi-Cultural Training in Psychology

The Cambridge Hospital Department of Psychiatry

The Danielsen Institute at Boston University

Edith Nourse Rogers Memorial Veterans Affairs Medical Center

Franciscan Children's Hospital and Rehabilitation Center

Harvard Medical School/Children's Hospital (formerly listed as Children's Hospital/Judge Baker Children's Center)

Harvard Medical School/ Massachusetts General Hospital

Harvard Medical School/ Massachusetts Mental Health Center

University of Massachusetts at Amherst Center for Counseling and Academic Development–Division of Counseling Psychology Services

University of Massachusetts Health Services–Mental Health Division

McLean Hospital/Harvard Medical School (formerly listed as McLean Hospital)

South Shore Mental Health Center, Inc.

Suffolk University Counseling Center

Tewksbury Hospital–Hathorne Mental Health Units

Veterans Affairs Medical Center

Westborough State Hospital

Westfield Area Mental Health Clinic

Worcester State Hospital

Worcester Youth Guidance Center

Michigan

Children's Hospital of Michigan

Community Mental Health Board

DMC Sinai-Grace Hospital (formerly listed as Sinai Hospital of Detroit)

Grand Valley State University–Career Planning and Counseling Center

Henry Ford Hospital Health Sciences Center (formerly listed as Henry Ford Hospital)

Henry Ford Wyandotte Hospital (formerly listed as Wyandotte Hospital and Medical Center)

John D. Dingell Veterans Affairs Medical Center (formerly listed as Veterans Affairs Medical Center, Allen Park, MI)

University of Michigan Institute for Human Adjustment

University of Michigan Internship Consortium

Michigan State University Counseling Center

Pine Rest Christian Mental Health Services

Veterans Affairs Health System (formerly listed as Veterans Affairs Medical Center)

Wayne State University School of Medicine–Department of Psychiatry and Behavioral Neurosciences

Western Michigan University–University Counseling and Testing Center

Minnesota

Children's Hospitals and Clinics (formerly listed as Minneapolis Children's Medical Center and as Children's Health Care, Inc.)

Federal Medical Center–U.S. Department of Justice, P.O. Box 4600

Hennepin County Medical Center

Human Services, Inc., in Washington County–Mental Health Division

University of Minnesota Counseling and Consulting Services

University of Minnesota Medical School (formerly listed as

University of Minnesota Psychology Internship Consortium)

University of St. Thomas Counseling and Career Services

Veterans Affairs Medical Center, Psychology Service (116B)

Mississippi

University of Mississippi Medical Center/VA Medical Center Consortium (formerly listed as University of Mississippi Medical Center/VA Medical Center–Jackson)

Mississippi State Hospital

Southern Mississippi Psychology Internship Consortium–University of Southern Mississippi Counseling Center

VA Gulf Coast Veterans Health Care System (formerly listed as Veterans Affairs Medical Center)

Missouri

Burrell Behavioral Health (formerly listed as Burrell Center)

Children's Mercy Hospital

University of Missouri–Columbia Counseling Service

Missouri Health Sciences Psychology Consortium (formerly listed as Mid-Missouri Psychology Internship Consortium)

University of Missouri–Kansas City Counseling and Testing Center

U.S. Medical Center for Federal Prisoners

Veterans Affairs Medical Center

Western Missouri Mental Health Center

Montana
Montana State University Counseling and Psychological Services

Nebraska
Nebraska Internship Consortium in Professional Psychology
Norfolk Regional Center

Nevada
Ioannis Lougaris Veterans Affairs Medical Center

New Hampshire
Dartmouth Medical School
University of New Hampshire Counseling Center
Riverbend Community Mental Health Services
Seacoast Mental Health Center, Inc.

New Jersey
CPC Behavioral Healthcare
Elizabeth General Medical Center–Department of Psychiatry
Greystone Park Psychiatric Hospital
Jersey Shore Medical Center
University of Medicine and Dentistry of New Jersey
Monmouth Medical Center
Trenton Psychiatric Hospital
Veterans Affairs New Jersey Health Care System

New Mexico
University of New Mexico Health Sciences Center (formerly listed as University of New Mexico School of Medicine)

Southwest Consortium Predoctoral Psychology Internship–Veterans Affairs Medical Center

New York
Albany Psychology Internship Consortium–Department of Psychiatry–Albany Medical College
Albert Einstein College of Medicine–Bronx Psychiatric Center
Association for the Help of Retarded Children
The Astor Home for Children
Beth Israel Medical Center
University at Buffalo/State University of New York (formerly listed as State University of New York at Buffalo)
The Center for Preventive Psychiatry
The Children's Village
Columbia-Presbyterian Medical Center–New York State Psychiatric Institute
Creedmoor Psychiatric Center
Crestwood Children's Center
Dutchess County Department of Mental Hygiene
Gouverneur Hospital–Department of Behavioral Health
Hudson River Regional Psychology Internship Program
Hutchings Psychiatric Center
Jewish Board of Family and Children's Services, Inc.
Jewish Child Care Association of New York
Karen Horney Clinic
Kings County Hospital Center

Lenox Hill Hospital
Lincoln Medical and Mental Health
Center
Long Island Jewish Medical Center
Maimonides Medical Center
Manhattan Psychiatric Center
Mount Sinai Medical Center
Nassau County Medical Center
New York Hospital–Cornell Medical
Center
New York University–Bellevue
Hospital Center
New York University Medical
Center–Rusk Institute of
Rehabilitation Medicine
North Bronx Healthcare Network
(formerly listed as North Central
Bronx Hospital)
North Shore University
Hospital–Cornell University
Medical College
Pace University–Counseling Center
Postgraduate Center for Mental
Health
Queens Children's Psychiatric Center
University of Rochester Counseling
and Mental Health Services
University of Rochester School of
Medicine and Dentistry
State University of New York Health
Science Center at Syracuse
St. Luke's/Roosevelt Hospital Center
St. Mary's Children and Family
Services
Stony Brook University/State
University of New York (formerly
listed as State University of New
York at Stony Brook)
Sunset Park Mental Health Center

VA Hudson Valley Healthcare
System (formerly listed as
Franklin Delano Roosevelt
Veterans Affairs Hospital)
Westchester Jewish Community
Services, Inc.

North Carolina
Broughton Hospital
Duke University Counseling and
Psychological Services
Duke University Medical Center
Federal Correctional Institution
University of North Carolina School
of Medicine
Veterans Affairs Medical Center

Ohio
University of Akron Counseling and
Testing Center
Applewood Centers, Inc.–Center for
Research, Quality Improvement,
and Training
Child and Adolescent Service Center
Children's Hospital, Inc.
Children's Hospital Medical Center
University of Cincinnati
Psychological Services Center
Louis Stokes Cleveland Department
of Veterans Affairs Medical Center
(formerly listed as Veterans
Affairs Medical Center)
Miami University Student
Counseling Service
Northeastern Ohio Universities
College of Medicine
Ohio State University Counseling
and Consultation Services
Wright-Patterson USAF Medical
Center

Wright State University–School of Professional Psychology–Ellis Institute

Oklahoma

Children's Medical Center
Northeastern Oklahoma Psychology Internship Program
Oklahoma Health Consortium (formerly listed as Oklahoma State Department of Health)
University of Oklahoma Health Sciences Center Internship Consortium

Oregon

Morrison Center
Oregon Health Sciences University Child Development and Rehabilitation Center
University of Oregon University Counseling Center
Tualatin Valley Mental Health Center
Veterans Affairs Medical Center

Pennsylvania

Allegheny General Hospital–Department of Psychiatry
The Child Guidance Center of the Children's Hospital of Philadelphia (formerly listed as Philadelphia Child Guidance Clinic)
Children's Seashore House of CHOP
The Devereux Foundation–Institute of Clinical Training and Research
Eastern Pennsylvania Psychiatric Institute, MCP Hahnemann University (formerly listed as Eastern Pennsylvania Psychiatric Institute/Allegheny University of the Health Sciences and as Medical College of Pennsylvania at Eastern Pennsylvania Psychiatric Institute) (Accredited, on probation status resulting from the program not having interns in 1999–2000.)
Friends Hospital–Department of Clinical Services
Norristown State Hospital–Psychology Department
Penn State Geisinger Medical Center (formerly listed as Geisinger Medical Center)
University of Pennsylvania–University Counseling Service
Pennsylvania Hospital (formerly listed as Institute of Pennsylvania Hospital)
Pennsylvania State University Center for Counseling and Psychological Services
Philhaven Hospital
University of Pittsburgh Counseling Center
Pittsburgh Veterans Healthcare System Internship (formerly listed as Pittsburgh Veterans Affairs Psychology Internship Consortium)
The Reading Hospital and Medical Center
Sarah A. Reed Children's Center
St. Francis Medical Center–Department of Psychology (Accredited, on probation status

resulting from the program not having interns in 1999–2000.)

Temple University Medical School

Western Psychiatric Institute and Clinic–Department of Psychiatry/ University of Pittsburgh School of Medicine

Widener University Internship–Institute for Graduate Clinical Psychology

Rhode Island

Brown University Clinical Psychology Internship Consortium

South Carolina

Medical University of South Carolina/VAMC Consortium–Department of Psychiatry

University of South Carolina Counseling and Human Development Center

William S. Hall Psychiatric Institute

South Dakota

Veterans Affairs Black Hills Health Care System (formerly listed as Fort Meade Veterans Affairs Medical Center West River Mental Health Center Psychology Internship Consortium)

Tennessee

The Guidance Center (formerly listed as Rutherford County Guidance Center)

James H. Quillen Veterans Affairs Medical Center

University of Memphis Center for Student Development (formerly listed as Memphis State University Center for Student Development)

University of Tennessee, Knoxville Student Counseling Services Center

University of Tennessee Professional Psychology Internship Consortium

Vanderbilt University–Veterans Affairs Medical Center

Veterans Affairs Medical Center

Texas

Austin State Hospital

Baylor College of Medicine–Department of Psychiatry and Behavioral Sciences

Central Texas Veterans Health Care System (formerly listed as Olin E. Teague Veterans Affairs Center)

Child and Family Guidance Center (formerly listed as Dallas Child Guidance Clinic)

Cypress-Fairbanks Independent School District–Department of Psychological Services

Dallas Public Schools (formerly listed as Dallas Independent School District)

Federal Medical Center (formerly listed as Federal Correctional Institution)

Fort Worth Independent School District

University of Houston Counseling and Psychological Services

Houston Independent School District

South Texas Veterans Health Care System (formerly listed as Audie

L. Murphy Memorial Veterans
Hospital)
Texas A&M University Student
Counseling Service
University of Texas at Austin
Counseling and Mental Health
Center (formerly listed as
University of Texas–Austin
Counseling, Learning, and Career
Services)
University of Texas Health Science
Center at San Antonio
The University of Texas Medical
Branch at Galveston
University of Texas Medical School
at Houston
University of Texas Southwestern
Medical Center at Dallas
Texas Tech University Counseling
Center
Texas Woman's University
Counseling Center
Veterans Affairs Medical Center
Wilford Hall Medical Center
(formerly listed as Wilford Hall
USAF Medical Center)

Utah
Brigham Young University
Counseling and Development
Center
Primary Children's Medical Center
University of Utah University
Counseling Center
Valley Mental Health (formerly listed
as Salt Lake Valley Mental Health)
Veterans Affairs Medical Center

Vermont
Fletcher Allen Health Care
Psychology Internship

Virginia
Alexandria Mental Health Center
Eastern Virginia Medical
School–Department of Psychiatry
and Behavioral Sciences
Federal Correctional Institution
McGuire Veterans Affairs Medical
Center
Medical College of Virginia/Virginia
Commonwealth University
Mount Vernon Center for Community
Mental Health
Naval Medical Center, Portsmouth
Veterans Affairs Medical Center
Virginia Beach City Public
Schools–Psychological Services
Programs for Exceptional
Children
University of Virginia Center for
Counseling and Psychological
Services
Virginia Commonwealth University
Counseling Services
Virginia Polytechnic Institute and
State University–University
Counseling Center
Virginia Treatment Center for
Children
Woodburn Center for Community
Mental Health

Washington
Spokane Mental Health (formerly
listed as Spokane Community
Mental Health Center)
Veterans Affairs Puget Sound Health
Care System–American Lake
Division
Veterans Affairs Puget Sound Health
Care System–Seattle Division

(formerly listed as Veterans Affairs Medical Center)

University of Washington School of Medicine–Clinical Psychology Internship Program

Washington State University Counseling Services

Western State Hospital–Department of Psychology

West Virginia

Federal Correctional Institution–U.S. Department of Justice

West Virginia University Carruth Center for Counseling and Psychological Services

West Virginia University Health Sciences Center–Department of Behavioral Medicine and Psychiatry

West Virginia University—Robert C. Byrd Health Sciences Center (formerly listed as West Virginia University School of Medicine)

Wisconsin

Aurora Behavioral Health Services/ Sinai Samaritan Medical Center

Clement J. Zablocki Veterans Affairs Medical Center

Ethan Allen School–Department of Health and Social Services

Mendota Mental Health Institute

Milwaukee County Mental Health Complex

University of Wisconsin Center for the Health Sciences

University of Wisconsin–Madison Counseling and Consultation Services

Wyoming

University of Wyoming Counseling Center

Wyoming State Hospital

Canada

Alberta Children's Hospital
Calgary, Alberta

Alberta Hospital Edmonton/Glenrose Rehabilitation Hospital Internship (formerly listed as Alberta Hospital Edmonton)
Edmonton, Alberta

British Columbia Children's Hospital
Vancouver, British Columbia

Centre for Addiction and Mental Health, Clarke Division (formerly listed as The Clarke Institute of Psychiatry)
Toronto, Ontario

Children's Hospital of Eastern Ontario
Ottawa, Ontario

Grand River Hospital (formerly listed as Kitchener-Waterloo Hospital)
Kitchener, Ontario

IWK-Grace Health Centre (formerly listed as IWK Children's Hospital)
Halifax, Nova Scotia

London Health Sciences Centre
London, Ontario

University of Manitoba Counseling Service
Winnipeg, Manitoba

University of Manitoba Faculty of Medicine
Winnipeg, Manitoba

McGill University Psychology
Internship Consortium
Department of Psychology
Montreal, Quebec

University of Ottawa
Centre for Psychological Services
School of Psychology
Ottawa, Ontario

The Ottawa Hospital–General Site
(formerly listed as Ottawa
General Hospital)
Ottawa, Ontario

Queen Elizabeth II Health Sciences
Centre (formerly listed as Camp
Hill Medical Centre)
Halifax, Nova Scotia

The Royal Ottawa Health Care Group
Ottawa, Ontario

Royal University Hospital–
Department of Clinical Health
Psychology
Saskatoon, Saskatchewan

Vancouver Hospital and Health
Sciences Centre–UBC Hospital
(formerly listed as University
Hospital–University of British
Columbia Site)
Vancouver, British Columbia

Workers Compensation Board of
British Columbia
Vancouver, British Columbia